During my interactions with Bobby I have found him to be very passionate about the church's mission for disciple-making. He is not just concerned that this happen in our gatherings. He is committed to seeing this happen in all of life. I'm grateful that he is applying his passion and experience to better equip the church to grow in discipleship in the home. I'm especially thankful to see a book coming out of his own experiences with his son. What a gift to have a father and son contribute out of their learning to further ours!

—Jeff Vanderstelt, visionary leader,
Soma Family of Churches

It has been my joy to know Dr. Bobby and to experience firsthand his passion for discipleship in this generation. *Dedicated* brings that passion into the home.

—Dr. K. P. Yohannan, founder and
international director, Gospel for Asia

A pesky question that is asked of most teachers is, "How do you help families do discipleship?" There are many answers. Frankly, however, most are disorganized and subjective. I like this book *Dedicated* because it is an organized answer based in experience. I like it because a father and son are involved and because I know that Bobby Harrington is the real deal as a man, husband, father, and pastor.

—Bill Hull, author, *Jesus Christ
Disciple Maker, The Disciple Making
Pastor,* and *The Disciple Making Church*

For years, parents have told us that the spiritual development of their children is their number one p̶ ̶ ̶ ̶ ̶ ̶ ̶ ̶ ̶ ̶ ̶ ̶ ̶ n a road map for how to make t̶ ̶ ̶ ̶ ̶ ̶ ̶ ̶ ̶ ̶ ̶ ̶ for every mom and dad.

—Bob Lep

*Dedicated* takes discipleship principles from the life of Jesus and from the Bible and shows parents how to apply them in the home. This book tells how every family can live with the blessing of God. It is a beautiful, down-to-earth story.

> —Dr. Robert Coleman, seminary professor; author, *The Master Plan of Discipleship*

Bobby Harrington is a man who understands that the mission of the church is to make disciples. He has spent the last several years helping leaders develop processes and strategies to do just that. He also is a man who has raised his kids to love and serve Jesus at the same time. His heart is to see every Christian become mature, and while the church plays a large part in that, he believes that every Christian parent's role is to disciple their own kids. Bobby and Chad have put together a book that will help parents invest in their children. I am excited about what this book can do for you and your family.

> —Jim Putman, senior pastor, Real Life Ministries

Passing on the faith within normal family structures has become the fastest growing omission in the contemporary church. This book is a practical guide to reintroduce this basic, relationally based, life-oriented catechesis into the life stream of the church. This is not just one of many important initiatives; the very future of the church depends on it!

> —Dr. Timothy C. Tennent, president, Asbury Theological Seminary

# DEDICATED

JASON HOUSER, BOBBY HARRINGTON,
AND CHAD HARRINGTON

# DEDICA✝ED

## TRAINING YOUR CHILDREN
## TO TRUST AND FOLLOW JESUS

ZONDERVAN

*Dedicated*
Copyright © 2015 by Dr. Bobby Harrington, Jason Houser, and Chad Harrington

This title is also available as a Zondervan ebook. Visit www.zondervan.com/ebooks.

Requests for information should be addressed to:
Zondervan, 3900 *Sparks Dr. SE, Grand Rapids, Michigan* 49546

ISBN 978-0-310-51829-7

*Cover design: Micah Kandros*
*Interior design: Matthew Van Zomeren*

*Printed in the United States of America*

15 16 17 18 19 20 21 22 23 24 /DCI/ 14 13 12 11 10 9 8 7 6 5 4 3 2 1

Bobby's Dedication:
*To the Lord and my family—*
*Cindy, Ashley, Chad, Mom, and Dad*

Jason's Dedication:
*To Housermania: Heidi, Ben, Brandon,*
*and Abby. I love you guys.*

Chad's Dedication:
*To Mom and Dad, who loved my sister and me*
*into the kingdom. Thank you for letting us choose God.*
*I am eternally grateful.*

# CONTENTS

# ACKNOWLEDGMENTS

**THE LORD HAS SURROUNDED US** with so many incredible people, and every victory in our lives would not be possible without these brothers and sisters in Christ.

Thank you, Ryan Pazdur, for your vision for this book and for your depth of insight throughout the editing process. It made this book so much better. And thanks to the rest of the team: Josh Blunt, Brian Phipps, and Robin Schmitt for flexing your editing skills as well.

*From Bobby*: special thanks to Jason for his partnership—so grateful that "my words were big in your ears" when you came to the church and you overlooked all of the shortcomings and tension in the writing process. Thank you, Chad, for overlooking my weaknesses and focusing on my strengths. I am grateful to Cindy, Ashley, and the faithful leaders (like Kathy Cawley) and the elders (David, Mike, Tony, and Ed) at Harpeth Community Church for supporting us. Special thanks for feedback on early material especially to Jen Taylor and those in the Dedicated Class—John and Gina Williams, Cam McLaughin, Jason Henderson, Karen Jackson, and Lyneve Fulton.

*From Chad*: special thanks to George Ezell, John Harmon, Shivraj Mahendra, Joe Hwang, Randy, Lyneve, and my family for support and input through the process. Thanks to Dad and Jason for putting up with a young buck like me and for the opportunity to join the project, not just help out. Your love and mercy made it possible for a father and a son to work together. Thanks to God for all the good.

*From Jason*: special thanks to Heidi, Ben, Brandon, and Abby for your sacrifices of time and attention as we worked through the creation and editing of this book. Thanks to both of you, Bobby and Chad. It takes courage to create a work like this as a father and son. I have admired your honesty and tenacity as we have climbed this mountain together. Thank you to my younger brother, Joshua Houser, and my brother in Christ Michael Martin for your partnership and constant encouragement. Thank you to the pastors at Lighthouse: Greg Fadness, Kevin Newbry, Ron Heath, and the amazing in-house editing Pastor Bryan Devore (for all the extra hours reading through this manuscript). And thanks to my partners in ministry and their families at Seeds Family Worship: Philip and Jessica Morlan, Joshua and Linda Houser, Darin and Joey Blood, Bryan and Stephanie Vignery, and Matthew and Jane Rowland.

# INTRODUCTION

**SHE WEPT BITTERLY.**

Hannah wanted a boy, but God had not granted her the gift of motherhood. For years and years she asked God for a son, but year after year she heard nothing. The silence was unbearable. She couldn't eat; she only wept. Tears flowed like a river.

Her prayer at the sanctuary was this: "God, if you give me a son, you can have him. He'll go into ministry—I'll make sure of it. If you give me a son, he's yours." She prayed with tears in her eyes, not sure if God was even listening.

One year, she went to the sanctuary to pray as usual. The tears started as she prayed in her heart, "God, if you give me a son, I'll give him back to you. I promise." Her lips moved, but no words came out. Her demeanor was odd enough that when the priest saw her, he thought she was drunk. He confronted her, but when she explained herself, he understood.

"May God answer your prayer and give you what you've asked of him," he said.

His words surprised her, but she held onto hope that God would give her a son.

Normally, she left her time of worship there with red eyes, but this year she left with a smile.

11

Sure enough, God answered her prayer with a yes and gave her a baby boy. As soon as she could take him out of their home, she and her husband brought him to the Lord's house to dedicate him to God. Her tears of mourning had become tears of joy. God had given her a son. When they arrived, she told the priest, "Sir, I am the woman who stood here praying to God. I prayed for this child, and God has given me what I asked of him. So now I am giving him back to God. For the rest of his life, he will be the Lord's."

◆　◆　◆

The story of Hannah's prayer and her dedication of her son is found in 1 Samuel chapter 1. Hannah and her husband, Elkanah, dedicated their son, Samuel, to God, and God used this boy to change history. Samuel poured his life into leading and guiding the nation of Israel as a prophet. He led them through difficult times. He anointed the nation's first king. His life was devoted to serving God's people.

But long before Samuel's life was given to serve God's purposes, Hannah herself was dedicated to God. She came to see that her future was in God's hands, and God worked in her heart to enable her to trust him completely. Before Samuel was ever born, Hannah had already laid him on the altar, ready to give what God had provided back to him.

Today it is popular for Christian parents to dedicate their children, much like Hannah and Elkanah did thousands of years ago. While the specific traditions and practices take on different forms for each family and church, the reason why parents do this is typically the same: they want God's best for their children. When new parents first hold their baby boy or girl, they know they have received a special gift, a gift that is theirs not to own but to invest in and ultimately to give back to the Lord. Out of gratitude to God, many parents bring their children to the church, placing them before God's people and committing them to the Lord.

# INTRODUCTION

What better way to begin the journey of parenting a child! As parents ourselves, we have dedicated each of our children and have found this practice to be a meaningful experience. Unfortunately, for many parents, the dedication of their child is just another event—a time for reflection and commitment perhaps, but there is little practical follow-up. Parents have good intentions when they dedicate their child, but they lack a plan for training them to follow Jesus.

We want more for our children—and yours. We've written this book to help you better understand what it means to dedicate your children to the Lord *every* day. Dedication is a way of life that we teach our kids, not just something we do at the beginning of a child's life.

The devastating reality that we must acknowledge is that many people who have been dedicated as children start out well, but they do not finish the race of faith. Some make bad choices and wander from the truth they have been taught. Others are following parents who have not dedicated themselves to the lifelong race required of people who follow Jesus. Parents who wish to raise dedicated children must first dedicate themselves to being disciples—committed followers of Jesus. Then they can pass on what they know and are learning to their kids—coaching their children.

Dedication comes down to one core issue for parents—living a discipleship lifestyle. A dedicated life involves being a disciple of Jesus and then making disciples of Jesus. But how do you do this? That's what this book is all about. We know it isn't easy to follow Jesus and teach your children to follow Jesus. We make mistakes. We fail. Our kids inevitably pick up some of our bad habits and sinful patterns. But despite these difficulties, Jesus calls us to follow him, and we must be dedicated to the task of learning from him and then teaching our children how to be dedicated to Christ as well. We invite you to join us in this journey as we go beyond the dedication ceremony.

We'll share our own struggles and victories along the way. Each of the three authors brings a unique perspective. Bobby, with his wife, Cindy, offers the perspective of an experienced father. Jason, with his wife, Heidi, gives us insight into the perspective of a younger father with children still at home. And Chad, Bobby and Cindy's son, offers the perspective of an adult child—what it's like to be raised in a home where your parents are dedicated to the Lord and have offered your life for God's purposes.

We want to note that the stories and examples of this book are written from a father's (or son's) perspective. While not always mentioned directly, our wives play an integral role in every aspect of our lives as parents, and every principle discussed in this book comes from our partnership with them. We also want to say to single parents that we have written with both married and single parents in mind (see also appendix 2).

One final word about the context for this book and how the book can be used. We understand that when it comes to raising children to follow Jesus, we aren't the first to write on this topic. And we know that various church traditions have differing approaches to issues like baptism and the involvement of children in the life of the church. Our goal in this book isn't to address these important theological concerns. Regardless of your particular tradition or background—however you "dedicate" children—we believe that the principles and lessons in this book will be helpful to you as you seek to raise a child dedicated to the Lord in every area of life. Though we come from church traditions that emphasize adult baptism by immersion and typically have a special dedication service for newborn children, feel free to adapt and apply this material to your context.

Before we get started, we want to remind you that spiritual parenting is a marathon, not a sprint, and the goal isn't to run fast; it's to persevere and finish the race. So we say to those who want to run this race well: You have dedicated your children to the Lord, which is the first step, but will you take it all the way and train your children to trust and follow Jesus for their entire lives?

# THREE DIFFERENT VOICES

The three of us (Bobby, Jason, and Chad) care about Christian discipleship, but for slightly different reasons. Chad is in his late twenties and doesn't yet have kids, but as Bobby's son, he can speak to the power of growing up in a family in which discipleship was modeled and taught. Jason is in his early forties with three kids and understands firsthand the challenges and joys of discipling kids today. He will speak to the importance of subjects like family worship and discipleship coaching. And Bobby, in his midfifties with two kids, is now a parent of adult children and serves as a pastor and disciple maker who teaches across North America on the topic of discipleship. We represent three generations, roughly fourteen years apart, and we write as friends and as disciples of Jesus.

CHAD: My earliest memories include a lot of time at the church—the first to arrive and the last to leave—because my dad is a pastor. We had family devotions, but the most important thing my parents did for me was to show me how to follow Jesus by being honest and real with me about their own walk with Jesus. At times, I struggled to own my faith—questioning God, the Bible, and the way of Jesus—but my parents remained gracious with me through my doubts. By the grace of God, I am a disciple of Jesus.

BOBBY: My wife, Cindy, and I have done our best to train our two children, Chad and Ashley, to be true disciples of Jesus Christ. Like all parents, we are fallible. I have been in full-time ministry for more than twenty-seven years, but I always considered my wife and my children my most important ministry. From the time Cindy was pregnant with Ashley, we became devoted students of parenting. We spent a lot of time looking to the Bible and to parents and grandparents who left a significant legacy of spiritual influence on their children and grandchildren.

JASON: I am a family pastor, songwriter, and father of a family that we call Housermania. Abby, our youngest, creates works of art out of whatever she can find. Brandon, our middle man, talks about his adventure for the day or shares his newest joke. And our oldest, Ben, is a teenager who spends time on his iPad searching for the latest and greatest in technology. Heidi, the mother of Housermania, holds all this madness together and still manages to work part-time as a nurse practitioner. Our marriage was redeemed and renewed during our time at the church where Bobby is the lead pastor. Following that miracle, the Lord started us on a journey called Seeds Family Worship, a national ministry whose mission is to "help families experience God's Word."

# CHAPTER 1

# DEDICATED TO DISCIPLESHIP

IN HIS BOOK *The Great Omission*, Dallas Willard describes "the great omission" in the Christian church today. It's a lack of discipleship.[1] Willard writes, "The governing assumption today, among professing Christians, is that we can be 'Christians' forever and never become disciples." Discipleship is the great omission of Jesus' Great Commission.

We often assume that discipleship is something the church does. Maybe it's a program or a small group we join. Perhaps it involves attending an adult education class or a weekend retreat. But discipleship is more than a program, a process, or an event. In fact, it's more than just something the church is responsible for. Discipleship begins with the family, and it is the core calling of Christian parents.

Let's start with a specific definition of discipleship. Some of the top discipleship leaders in the country, in collaboration with Discipleship.org, came together and created a definition that we believe is biblically solid and simple:

Discipleship is helping people to trust and follow Jesus.[2]

Matthew 28:18–20 is a great source for this definition. It serves as a helpful framework for understanding what the Bible teaches about discipleship (or "disciple making"). The verse is easy to remember, and we encourage you to memorize it: "Then Jesus came to them and said, 'All authority in heaven and on earth has been given to me. Therefore go and make disciples of all nations, baptizing them in the name of the Father and of the Son and of the Holy Spirit, and teaching them to obey everything I have commanded you. And surely I am with you always, to the very end of the age.'"

This passage, commonly referred to as the Great Commission, gives us a framework for discipleship. It is based on what Jesus had been doing with his disciples over the course of three years of ministry together. Now, before he ascended to his Father, he told them to go and do for others what he had been doing for them. They would have immediately understood what he was asking them to do. Because Jesus did everything in the context of relationships. His teaching, his ministry, his patterns of daily life—all of these were lived out before his followers. In many ways, the relationship between a teacher and his disciples is similar to the close relationship between a child and his or her parents, so we as parents can learn from Jesus as the master teacher.

This text reveals four key elements to making disciples.

1. *Helping people.* We have to initiate and be intentional because we are to "go" and "make" disciples (v. 19).
2. *Trust.* Disciple making is about repentance and conversion with the accent on grace: "baptizing them in the name of the Father and of the Son and of the Holy Spirit" (v. 19). Baptism represents our acceptance of a new life, where we rely on the grace of Jesus Christ.
3. *Follow.* Disciple making is also about obedience and sanctification (increasing holiness): "teaching them to obey everything I have commanded you" (v. 20).

4. *Jesus.* Jesus is the object and focus of discipleship. He does not leave us on our own, trying to accomplish all of this by ourselves, because he promises to be personally present for the entire process, with us to the end.

Again, our definition for discipleship is *helping people to trust and follow Jesus.* When it comes to parenting, there is a specific, important focus. Two key passages define what a dedicated parent is.

Ephesians 6:4: "Fathers, do not exasperate your children; instead, bring them up in the *training* and instruction of the Lord" (emphasis added).
Proverbs 22:6: "*Train* up a child in the way he should go; even when he is old he will not depart from it" (ESV, emphasis added).

These passages emphasize that dedicated parents train their children to trust and follow Jesus. So with these verses in mind, we have taken our definition of discipleship, added an emphasis on training, and applied it to parenting.

Discipleship for dedicated parents is *training your children to trust and follow Jesus.*

This is a simple definition but not a simplistic one. The full meaning of it is wonderfully life-altering, and we will develop it as we work through the rest of this book.

# FAMILY DISCIPLESHIP

In his 2005 book *Soul Searching*, author and sociologist Christian Smith points out that only a third of families with teens talk together about God, the Scriptures, prayer, or other religious or spiritual matters a few times a week or more.[3] When I (Bobby) was raising my children, the research showed that God, the Bible,

JASON: My wife, Heidi, and I laugh when we look back at the beginning of our family. I remember that day like it was yesterday, leaving the hospital when our first child was born. Benjamin—our seven-pound, two-ounce little boy—felt like he weighed one hundred pounds in his car seat as I carried him for the first time down the hallway of Baptist Hospital in Nashville, Tennessee.

There was a tsunami of emotions swirling in my mind as the gravity of parenting fully hit me: *We don't have the first clue about how to raise a child!* Walking out of that hospital with him that afternoon reminded me of how I felt the time I went bungee jumping off a three-hundred-foot tower. I had a few butterflies in my stomach beforehand, but the second I took the leap of faith, my heart screamed, *Maybe you should have put a little more thought into this decision!*

In those initial moments as a parent, it felt like the heaviest weight of parenting was the responsibility of keeping our son alive. I hadn't even begun to consider the spiritual responsibility of raising a son. Thankfully, the Lord had a plan to take care of Benjamin both physically and spiritually. Not only was parenthood a massive life-change for Heidi and me; the Lord used it as a catalyst for a spiritual awakening in our lives.

or religious things were seldom discussed in most homes. Only 10 percent of church families discussed faith with any degree of regularity; in 43 percent of homes in the denominations surveyed, faith was never discussed.[4] George Barna's 2003 research demonstrated that "in a typical week, fewer than 10 percent of parents who regularly attend church with their kids read the Bible together, pray together (other than at meal times), or participate in an act of service as a family unit."[5] It is hard to find up-to-date statistics. But in my experience as a pastor today—including the extensive networking that I do to help churches around the nation with discipleship—I believe that there is even less discipleship going on in the homes of churchgoing families today. Very few children and teens are experiencing regular Bible reading and devotions at home. Very few parents are actively discipling their children.

Both of these studies identify parental influence as the most significant factor in the spiritual development of children. In his study, Smith comments, "A lot of research in the sociology of religion suggests that the most important social influence in shaping young people's religious lives is the religious life modeled and taught to them by their parents."[6] But the statistics also show that many parents are failing to model a life of discipleship for their children. We cite these statistics not to discourage you or cause you to throw this book aside and give up but to help you as a parent to understand that you are not alone in your struggle.

Parents need a realistic understanding of what it means to be a spiritual parent, where they count the costs and plan for the long haul if they want to be successful. The basic definition of a spiritual parent is this: a parent who makes the spiritual well-being of their children their top priority. Again, this isn't easy; it's both difficult and challenging. Still, the reward is great. And remember, you aren't alone. You will have the power, inspiration, and help of the creator of the universe.

## WHY READ THIS BOOK?

In his classic book on family discipleship, *Faith Training*, Joe White gives a wonderful visionary picture of what it looks like to train your children to trust and follow Jesus. White tells of his time with Gene Stallings at Texas A&M. Stallings went on to become the coach of the Alabama Crimson Tide and eventually led them to win the national championship. Upon hearing the news that Stallings had been selected as the national coach of the year, White called Stallings to congratulate him. Stallings responded with humility, saying to White, "If you want to measure my success as a man, don't look at my win-loss record. Look at my kids, and see how well they're doing with the Lord."[7]

White then recounted another conversation with Stallings. "I quickly recalled a conversation Coach and I had when he was with the Dallas Cowboys a few years ago. He asked me that day what my goal in life was. I told him it was to live for Christ. He replied abruptly, 'That's not mine.' I said, 'What is yours, then?' He took a pencil and wrote down the following numbers: 29, 30, 31. Then he shoved the paper to my side of his desk and explained, 'When my kids are 29, 30, 31, I want them to be godly people with godly kids in godly homes.' "[8]

Stallings nailed it! As successful as he was in the realm of athletic coaching, he understood that at the end of the day, his role as a parent was far more important than his career. Stallings could have easily neglected his role as a father to pursue a high-profile career in coaching, but he understood that God had given him three children, and he was the one responsible for discipling them and teaching them to follow Jesus.

The truth is that if we succeed in finance, teaching, or even ministry but fail at home, we will have failed in one of our primary, God-given responsibilities. Being a mom or dad may not have been one of your life goals when you were younger, but now that you have children, you've been given that privilege. Stallings understood that his success was based not on how well he did on the field but on what he modeled in the home.

Is the same true for you?

# DEDICATION IN ACTION

*This section in each chapter is to help you process the content along the journey. The last point, "Listen," refers to a Seeds Family Worship song, which you can download online at* seedsfamilyworship. com.

REMEMBER. Have you ever decided to publicly dedicate your children to the Lord? Take some time to read the story of Hannah and Samuel again in 1 Samuel 1. If you have never considered dedicating your children to God, take a moment to think about this commitment and discuss it with your spouse, if possible.

CONSIDER. As you think about your role as a parent, recall the definition of discipleship we gave you earlier: *Discipleship (for parents) is training your children to trust and follow Jesus.* Spend some time reflecting on each aspect of this definition and how it applies to your parenting.

PRAY. Take time now to ask the Lord to show you how he wants you to be a dedicated parent as you read the book.

RESPOND. How is the Holy Spirit leading you *today* to live out your dedication to God in discipleship?

LISTEN. "Go" (Matt. 28:19), *The Power of Encouragement,* Seeds Family Worship.

# CHAPTER 2

# DEDICATED TO RELATIONSHIPS

THE RELATIONSHIP between a parent and a child can be one of the deepest and most intimate relationships we experience in life. As a parent, you see how your child's life begins, how he or she grows and develops, and you have a hand in shaping and guiding their choices. And yet, as every parent knows, there are no guarantees that children will follow what you say to them or that they will listen to your advice. Having a close and healthy relationship with your kids isn't automatic. I (Bobby) learned this truth the hard way. The truth is that if our children know that we love them, and if we regularly invest in developing a close relationship with them, they will want to listen to us and learn from us. They will learn to trust us and believe that we really want what's best for them.

This was a profound insight for me as my children were growing up. In part, this was because I had experienced the opposite with my own father. As a young child, I was very close to my dad. I knew he loved me, but as I entered elementary school, his workaholism and alcoholism got the best of him. He was too busy for a close relationship with me. Sometimes he would be out drinking and would return home violent or hungover. Since those years, my father has changed his ways, and I know he truly wanted to care for me, but all I knew during my childhood was that he was caught up in his own issues.

It's hard for a child to describe his feelings toward a father he respects and wants to please but who never shows up for hockey and soccer games. It is hard to listen to a man when you don't believe he really cares about you, especially when he is violent at home. Even the many wonderful things he does come through with a mixed message. I knew, as I grew older, that I didn't want to follow my dad or treat my son the way he treated me, and my heart grew hard toward him.

When I was in my early twenties, my dad repented and gave his life to Christ. And he truly changed. Over time, he was able to restore many things that had been lost in his relationship with my mom, my sisters, and me. A few years after he became a follower of Jesus, I had the privilege of working with him at his trucking company. We restored the love and closeness we had when I was a young boy, but I continued to struggle with my bitterness and resentment toward him. It remained difficult for me to learn from him, to follow his example, and to listen to his advice.

The impact of a parent cannot be overestimated. It has great power to teach a child to follow Jesus, but because of sin, it also has the power to bring damage and pain. Today I am grateful that God redeemed my father. Over the years, he has pursued me and built a relationship with my wife and my children. My children can now look at the legacy of his marriage, one that has lasted more than sixty years through many challenges and struggles. Our family history is filled with brokenness and heartache, yet it is also a story of repentance, restoration, and a lasting legacy.

When I became a dad, I determined that, with God as my helper, my children would not have the same experience I had growing up.

I made it a point to bend heaven and earth to be there for them. I made a decision, when they were first born, to dedicate myself to them, even if it meant that sometimes people would not see me as a good pastor. I ordered my priorities to be a Christian husband, then to be the best father I could be, and to let everything else fit in after that. In our home, we sought to put relationships first.

In the previous chapter, we talked about the importance of discipleship. But we want to emphasize that discipleship is more than a program or something you do with your children before each meal. Discipleship is *relational*, which involves all of life. Having a strong relationship with your children is the basis of your influence as you disciple them.

That said, we need to recognize the reality that our modern culture and many of our technological advancements are working against our desire to have healthy, close family relationships. Microsoft's Linda Stone has referred to our culture and time as the age of "continuous partial attention."[1] Our families are busy doing many things, yet often we are only partially present for them. As a parent, you may work sixty hours a week, and then you spend a few nights at home alone with the kids. But think about what you are doing during that time. Are you fully present, or are you tired and preoccupied with other things? This isn't just a problem for busy parents. Many of our young children are growing up fixated on smart phones and apps. They spend more time in front of a screen than they do talking with and listening to other family members. You will see a mother talking on the phone while her children eat dinner, or a father watching television with his children, oblivious to the people in the room with him.

Though each generation has its own challenges, it is fair to say that history has never seen a society quite like ours, in which both mom and dad are working full-time jobs while juggling the complexities of life. Our families exist on the border of chaos.

CHAD: I was blessed to witness firsthand the fruit of my grandfather's repentance. The change in his life was real, and it was visible in his relationships within our family. I remember when my grandfather first shared our family story with me from beginning to end. He's a great storyteller, and while he spoke, I began to grasp the depth of his struggle with alcohol. My grandfather was a hardworking and successful businessman, but he was truly addicted. His addiction led him to neglect relationships. He worked hard to provide for his family physically, but he didn't know how to develop healthy relationships with them, let alone disciple them.

Talking with my grandfather helped me understand my dad as well. Though my dad had a rough childhood, it's amazing to look at who he has become. He didn't learn how to be a spiritual parent from his father; he and my mom took the challenge of discipling my sister and me in the ways of Jesus, learning all of this from scratch. They didn't always get it right, but I definitely benefited from their efforts, especially their choice to develop a relationship with me in practical ways.

Even if your family background is rough and filled with pain and brokenness, don't lose hope. God can break the chains of sin between generations.

Our American culture is often opposed to the goals and concerns of biblical parenting. Today we struggle to slow down and focus enough to really know people, even those in our own family, the people we live with.

The good news is that we don't have to succumb to our culture. You can be different! And in the process of raising your children to follow God, he will transform your life and the life of your family, helping you to become more relational and love your children with depth and intimacy like Jesus loves us.

# JESUS AND RELATIONSHIP

Jesus gives us the best model for discipleship. He spent time with his disciples by listening to their needs, addressing the questions they had, and speaking to the issues they faced as he walked with them on the road from village to village. On one such occasion, Jesus and his disciples were traveling through Galilee, and they arrived at the village of Capernaum, where Peter lived on the coast of the Sea of Galilee (Mark 9:33–37). The walk was a twenty-five-mile journey, so they had plenty of time to talk. And Jesus had plenty of time to listen as well. After overhearing an argument between several of his followers, he took the opportunity to ask his disciples about it. At first they were quiet, perhaps even embarrassed. Jesus used this teachable moment to help them better understand what life is like when lived before God, under his guidance and authority—the kingdom life of a disciple. Jesus said, "If anyone would be first, he must be last of all and servant of all" (v. 35 ESV). Gathering up a child in his arms, he added, "Whoever receives one such child in my name receives me, and whoever receives me, receives not me but him who sent me" (v. 37 ESV).

Examples like this fill the Gospels. The New Testament has many stories of how Jesus spent time with his disciples, listening to them and teaching them in the context of life together. In these accounts, we observe at least three aspects of relational discipleship. We learn that Jesus

- *spent time* with his disciples,
- *listened* to his disciples,
- *spoke truth* into his disciples' lives.

The walk from Caesarea to Capernaum is a long trip on foot. I realize that you may not take your children on many twenty-five-mile hikes, but I'm willing to bet you will have a few road trips together as a family. Learn to redeem these times. As you *spend time together*, you have a unique opportunity to ask questions, to learn what your children are thinking about. Don't just plug in the movie or let the kids listen to music for a thousand miles. The key is to look for opportunities to engage your children, to make the most of these ordinary moments when you are together, just like Jesus did with his disciples.

Our tendency is to overlook these times, to focus on the planned and programmed times—which are important, of course. But don't dismiss these road trip conversations as unimportant. Jesus *listened* to his disciples so that he understood them and knew where they were. Most children, after some prompting, will reveal what they are struggling with. It may come through in their tone, even without any prompting, if you'll just listen. Jesus listened to his disciples so that he knew how to respond to them. And like Jesus, we need to be on the lookout for these moments, times when we can listen to our kids and better understand their concerns, their hopes, dreams, and desires.

In addition to listening, Jesus *taught* his disciples an important truth about life—that his way of life is opposite the way of the world: "If anyone would be first, he must be last of all and servant of all." To the disciples, this must have sounded crazy! Notice that Jesus didn't wait for a formal time in the synagogue to teach. He didn't delegate the teaching to someone else. He seized the opportunity he had on a long road trip and turned it into a teachable moment. He was aware of others and ready to speak into their lives.

As we said earlier, relationships are the context in which spiritual parenting happens. But relationships get messy. You may be dealing with a disobedient child who is rebelling against you. Or you may be struggling with anger in your own heart because of something a child has said or done. Discipleship happens between a parent and a child, but it's not always perfect. Sometimes it involves honestly talking about mistakes or admitting something done wrong and asking for forgiveness. But if you make the relationship the priority, it sets you up to be effective when you attempt to give direction and instruction in a more formal way, perhaps through a Bible study or family devotion. When your children feel secure in their relationship with you, they will be more receptive to the truth you want to convey to them. And you will get a front-row seat as you watch God change their hearts.

# RELATIONSHIP AND RULES

What do we mean by a relational approach to parenting? A relational approach can be contrasted with parenting approaches that tend to rely more on a parent's positional authority or a program of rules and expectations that guide family interactions. A priority on relationship requires a delicate balance, particularly in working through the tension between relationship and discipline.

Several years ago, I (Bobby) heard Josh McDowell teach a framework that helped me better understand how rules and relationship work together. In the first scenario, let's consider a family in which there are clear rules and guidelines for the home, but the relationship between the child and his parents isn't close. This arrangement will typically lead a child to rebel against authority. We can summarize it with this simple question:

Rules - Relationship = Rebellion

Parents who focus on simply enforcing the rules, adopting a legalistic approach with their children, will tend to raise rebellious kids. The rules may be enforced in the home, but they aren't explained and often do not lead to healthy, loving relationships. This approach often produces anger in children, whether or not the parents are aware of the cause. The Bible describes this as *exasperation*, making kids unnecessarily angry. In Ephesians 6:4, Paul writes, "Fathers, do not exasperate your children; instead, bring them up in the training and instruction of the Lord." Parents who tell their kids what to do but don't develop a close relationship with them create an environment for anger and resentment to grow. The rules often come across as unfair, unneeded, and unwanted.

In some families, the opposite approach has become more the norm. Increasingly in our culture, parents have rejected rules and structure, preferring to be "friends" with their children. This parenting approach often centers on what a child wants, giving the child the freedom to make his or her own choices. But such an approach inevitably leads to unwise choices and a reckless approach to life. We could summarize it with this equation:

Relationship - Rules = Recklessness

Parents who want to be "friends" or "buddies" with their children but fail to provide the appropriate leadership and discipline for kids often cause their children to be morally reckless. Children raised in a purely relational home are likely to take advantage of their parents. Because the parents do not consistently discipline their kids and establish rules, the children fail to learn self-control or respect for authority.

As you can see, when proper rules are not established or a relationship is absent, the home is unstable and full of problems. However, there is another way, a balanced approach that acknowledges the importance of appropriate rules while prioritizing the necessity of a grace-based relationship:

Relationship + Rules = Righteousness

Parents who learn to spend time with their kids and develop a healthy relationship with them while also providing appropriate boundaries and rules will, by God's grace, see the fruit of righteousness in their children. Teaching your children to live righteously isn't a mathematical formula, of course. It is the result of the Lord's grace. The fruit that God grows in the lives of our children comes from the seeds we plant as they grow and mature, seeds established through discipline within the context of relationship. We will discuss the concept of biblical discipline in a later chapter, but for now we want to point out that discipline can be a wonderful tool for discipleship when it happens in the context of a loving, grace-filled relationship.[2]

Emphasizing to parents the need for relationship is important now more than ever because of the increase in broken family relationships. The parent-child relationship has always been important, but as a culture, we're losing. We've replaced life-giving relationships with schedules and technology, trying to achieve our own goals. If we want to change the culture, we need to start in our own homes.

Like Jesus, the apostle Paul embodied this kind of intimate, relational love when he wrote as a spiritual parent to the church of Thessalonica, "You know how, *like a father with his children*, we exhorted each one of you and encouraged you and charged you to walk in a manner worthy of God, who calls you into his own kingdom and glory" (1 Thess. 2:11–12 ESV, emphasis added). Paul makes it clear that good parents invest in their children by nourishing them, not exasperating them. We encourage and exhort our children toward godliness, giving them a vision of what it means to walk worthy of God. We challenge them by calling them to a different way of life, but not in a way that shames them or creates bitterness. Clearly, there are boundaries in this type of interaction, but the goal is growth and maturity.

# INVESTING IN THE RELATIONSHIP

You are a spiritual parent. God has placed you over your children, and you will find that relational discipleship in the home takes time. It's not going to happen overnight. You cannot expect to build a Christ-centered relationship with your children without investing time into them. As daunting as this can seem at first, keep in mind that it can take on many different forms. Let's get a bird's-eye view of several ways you can spend time with your family in various contexts of life.

## Invest Quality Time

It's helpful to differentiate between *quality* time and *quantity* of time. We advocate spending both with your kids. The truth is that quality moments happen most naturally as you spend a lot of time together. In other words, it's difficult to get quality without quantity.

When Chad was a boy, I (Bobby) spent a lot of time doing things with him like playing hockey in the garage or throwing a football in the yard. Jason spends time creating with his daughter Abby, joining her in painting a picture or sitting down beside her to listen as she explains her latest work of art.

There's a time for watching and encouraging your child's talents and hobbies, but some of the best moments happen when you jump in and participate too. George Barna, author

JASON: I remember one evening when Abby brought home a large folder with her artwork from an entire semester in her art class. She invited me to look at her paintings and drawings with her. In that moment, I realized that I had missed many of these moments in the past, being too caught up in the busyness of life. God gave me grace to say yes and respond to her invitation, and the two of us sat together and enjoyed all of her sketches and paintings of flowers, animals, blue sky, and sunshine. I had a rare opportunity to see God's creativity flowing from my little girl's heart, and I was able to verbally affirm the gift that the Lord had given her to bring these pictures to life. Moments like these are sweet blessings for a parent and life-giving nourishment for a child's heart.

of *Revolutionary Parenting*, says that "revolutionary" parents—those who seek to make an eternal impact on their children—spend 90 to 120 minutes with their children per day.[3] We understand that most parents today do not do that; it's a high bar! Still, we recommend that parents begin to look at how they can realign their schedules to free up additional hours to be with their children. This might mean spending less time at work, less time pursuing your own hobbies, or less time making your house look perfect. Trust us, it's time you will not regret losing to be with your kids.

## Be Intentional

Joe White's book *Faith Training*, which we mentioned earlier, is one of the best books we have read on discipling your children. In it, Joe repeatedly talks about investing in relationships with your children: "I'll stop here to repeat the words of a friend that changed my parenting focus forever: The relationship is everything. (During times of fatigue and stress, I've repeated it over and over to myself a thousand times.) *The relationship is everything. The relationship is everything.*"[4]

We know that it is so tempting for parents to disengage after a long, hard day. We often feel we have nothing left to give to our families. And it's okay to feel this way, but we must not let these feelings alone dictate our actions and determine how we respond. We encourage you to build the habit of taking "just five minutes." Press through your feelings of exhaustion and spend just five minutes with your kids when you first come home. Some evenings you will experience those "moments of invigoration" that White describes. The five minutes you commit to your child can quickly turn into thirty or sixty minutes, and the time playing or talking together will be refreshing for you. There will be some times when it's a bit more work, and it is also wise to plan time together simply for the sake of maintaining healthy relationships. For example,

BOBBY: When my two children were in high school, I was pastoring and attending seminary. Our schedules were tight, and Cindy and I would occasionally stop and evaluate how things were going. We often circled back to one of our core values: Family relationships come first. There were times when we made some hard calls. I remember asking my kids to cancel plans they had made with friends to stay home for "family night." We established this pattern while Chad and Ashley were still young, so they didn't really push back against the expectation as they got older. It's easier to weave these habits into the fabric of your family if you establish them early and are consistent and clear. We knew we were asking our children to make a sacrifice for their family, but they did it willingly. They did it because they knew what our family valued and they wanted to honor their parents in this way.

CHAD: Looking back at our family nights, we often played games together. The games were fun and sometimes frustrating—because there was the difficulty of learning a new game, frustrations we had with each other, and some of us weren't good losers—but over time, we developed a culture of playing *together* as a family. Now when we get together, it's the norm, something we look forward to. I'm so thankful for times like these that we've had over the years, just hanging out together.

Bobby and Cindy did this by scheduling weekly family nights when their children were young and playing board games together, watching a movie as a family, or enjoying a favorite meal together.

Remember, being dedicated parents will often mean choosing the narrow, more difficult road. Disciple making is intentional work. Every relationship has those moments when you choose to love even when you aren't "feeling it." But we want to encourage you to just do it. Commit to it, build the habit, and the feelings will often follow. Then build in other habits as well—perhaps a monthly "date" with each child, a daily story time, or a yearly vacation. If you don't schedule these family times, you will soon find that school, work, and sports obligations swallow up your time. Choose the ways you want to develop relationship with your kids, and build those into the rhythm of your life.

## Learn Their Language, Enter Their World

Each of us expresses and receives love in different ways. One of the most helpful things you can do as a family is to talk about the unique and varied ways in which each family member likes to give and receive love. This is what author Gary Chapman has called the "love languages."[5] He lists five primary languages that people "speak."

- Words of affirmation
- Physical touch
- Quality time
- Acts of service
- Receiving gifts

For some of your children, words of affirmation, sincere compliments spoken aloud, are, more than anything else, what make them feel secure and appreciated. For others, it might be a gift you give or physical touch, a hug or a hand on a shoulder.

Some of your children will value intentional acts of service, like help folding their laundry or cooking their favorite food. There are also kids who like it when you spend special time with them.

Of course, we all appreciate all of these things, but each of us will naturally tend to express love in our preferred love language. It's likely that at least one of your children will experience and express love differently than you do, and it's your responsibility and privilege to learn their language and speak it regularly.

I (Jason) can see God's sense of humor (and his sanctification plan for me) in knowing that both my wife and oldest son Ben both share "quality time" as their primary love language. As an overcommitter and a traveling minister, I have often wished that "receiving gifts" was their love language. That way whenever I was gone or running late, I could just bring them an awesome gift and everything would be great!

Recently, my wife asked me what I thought our middle son Brandon's love language is, and I showed her a video from his last birthday party. It was obvious to her that it was "gifts" when she watched him open his presents—he was so full of joy that his face lit up like the Fourth of July. As for our little girl, her love language is physical touch, without a doubt. She will come up to me unannounced, give me a big hug, and say, "I love you, Daddy." Every child has a way they prefer to show and receive love. Your job is to find out by observation and dialogue what they like. Then you can keep that knowledge as your secret device to love them in extravagant ways.

## Get Away

One way to spend time with your kids is to invest in them away from the home too. Family vacations can be a great opportunity for discipleship. Consider your children's age and interests (and your budget) to choose an adventure that works for you. We've enjoyed trips that combine physical activity with extended time together—hiking, skiing, walking along the beach—but it's not necessary to travel very far or spend a lot of money to make special memories. A "staycation" full of picnics, day trips, and neighborhood bike rides can create just as much family time, without many expenses. Some of my (Jason) best memories as a child were going to Redfish Lake several summers in a row. If you've

CHAD: Every summer, our family spent at least a week at Sylvan Lake, water-skiing, swimming, and playing in the yard. Everything had a distinct sort of mystery to it. We had the freedom to explore the water, skip rocks, and buy whatever we wanted at the candy shop. It was a magical place. I don't remember any "spiritual" talks my mom or dad gave us at Sylvan Lake. We simply enjoyed life together. These are the experiences that develop memories and deepen relationships within the family. Trust is established, and that trust, developed over time, will give parents the ability to speak truth into the lives of their children when the moment is right. These extended times together stored up "chips in the bank," so that later, when things grew difficult, we were able to continue relating in healthy ways.

never been there, Redfish is a breathtakingly beautiful lake nestled in the mountains of Idaho. I can remember riding our bicycles together as a family down narrow dirt trails and meandering through the Rocky Mountain pines. I learned as a child that there was something special about our family disconnecting from the daily responsibilities of life and spending time together. Several years ago, we began creating new memories at Redfish Lake with our own children, and during the time we were there, my childhood memories were still as fresh as the mountain air.

## Grow with Them

Most dating or courting relationships involve some form of relational pursuit. Typically, when a man is interested in a woman, he pursues her — asking her out on a date and planning activities for them to do together. His pursuit is an expression of his interest, his desire to know this woman, and is essential for the relationship to grow. If he does not pursue the relationship, it is unlikely to grow or develop. Recall that our definition of disciple making

39

involves intentionality ("training"). The intentionality of pursuing a relationship applies to parenting as well as dating; we must pursue our children in order to help them grow.

This is what God does for us through Jesus. The good news of the gospel is that God has come in the person of Jesus Christ, our bridegroom, who pursues and redeems his bride, the church, and saves her from her sin, restoring people he loves to relationship with him.

God also pursues us as a loving Father, initiating a relationship with us through the Holy Spirit and adopting us into his family as his sons and daughters. Following the pattern of God, parents must also be intentional about pursuing their children. In fact, oftentimes God pursues relationship with our children through us.

When kids are small, they will gladly spend time with their parents, even just to run errands or help in the kitchen. However, as kids get older, you must pursue them more on their terms, not yours. Instead of inviting your children into activities you like, you will need to spend time doing activities they like. Instead of fitting time with them into your schedule, you might have to fit into their schedule!

In the end, pursuing your children — learning a love language, spending regular time together, and making sacrifices — is an opportunity to embody God's love the way Jesus did, when he "made his dwelling among us" and became one of us to pursue us (John 1:14). Discipling our children means entering their world and showing them, by example, how to follow Jesus.

## YOUR AIM

As a parent, one of the greatest revelations I (Jason) have had is this: no matter where I work, or whom I lead, or how many people I am responsible for, there is always someone else who can come and replace me and fill that role, probably better than me. It's humbling to admit this, but it is absolutely true.

But there is an exception to this. There is only one man among the billions of people on earth who can be the father of Ben, Brandon, and Abby Houser; and my wife, Heidi, is the only woman who can nurture them as their mother. These are the children God has entrusted to us, the ones God has given to us to nurture, train, and raise to trust and follow Jesus. We are the most influential voices in their lives, by God's design. Knowing this should motivate us to realign our calendars and commitments to connect with God's purposes.

So here is my question for you today: What are you doing to spiritually parent your children? It's tempting for us to parent on autopilot and let the church or the school raise our children, but the truth is that God has given us that responsibility. And not only are we to parent them; we are responsible for *spiritually* parenting them, teaching them what it means to trust and follow Jesus, praying for them and teaching them to respond to the good news of the gospel. Any sacrifices you make to do this will be worth it in the end. God promises us that none of our efforts will be wasted.

## DEDICATION IN ACTION

REMEMBER. In which ways did your parent(s) (or perhaps a mentor) spend time with you to develop a relationship? Also, what are your children's love languages? You can find more information and even take a low-cost or free survey to discover your or your children's love languages at *www.5lovelanguages.com*.

CONSIDER. Close relationships in the home establish the foundation for effective discipleship. If you are not *intentionally* spending time with your children, you will have a difficult time teaching them to trust and follow Jesus.

PRAY. Ask the Lord to show you creative and practical ways you can invest into your children. Ask for his help as you commit to cultivating a deeper relationship with them.

RESPOND. How is the Holy Spirit leading you *today* to live out your dedication to God in relationships?

LISTEN. "Genuine" (Rom. 12:9–11), *The Word of God*, Seeds Family Worship.

# CHAPTER 3

# DEDICATED TO SPIRITUAL PARENTING

**IT WAS A PERFECT, BLUE-SKY SUMMER** afternoon when I (Jason) received one of those unexpected phone calls that every parent fears. It was my younger brother, Joshua. He was trying to catch his breath on the other end of the line, and I could hear the panic in his voice as he relayed to me that my son Brandon had been in an accident. My wife and I needed to get to the emergency room at St. Luke's Hospital as soon as possible.

Heidi and I were at home getting ready to leave for a vacation. We had a few more errands to run before heading out to join the rest of our family. We'd decided to let our three kids travel on ahead of us with their grandparents and cousins. That's when the call came.

Talking with my brother, I learned what had happened. As the adults were unpacking for the weekend, the kids had sped off on a couple of new four-wheelers. Our son and his younger cousin had lost control of the quad when Brandon hit the gas instead of the brake. Shooting ahead, they had run into a barbed wire fence, which cut into Brandon's neck and face.

My brother and I prayed together on the phone as he rushed Brandon to the hospital. Heidi and I cried out to God that he would save our son's life: *Please, God, help him be okay. Please, have mercy on us!* My brother was afraid Brandon was going into shock, so he asked to talk to my wife, who is a nurse practitioner. I remember her asking how much he was bleeding, and my heart sank beneath the weight of every word. I prayed again, *Lord, please help us not to lose our little boy.*

We arrived at the ER at the same time as my brother, and together we carefully helped Brandon out of the van, blood running down his face from wounds on his eye and neck. Praying, we carried our six-year-old through the sliding door of the ER.

The Lord had great mercy on all of us that day; the punctures from the barbed wire fence missed both Brandon's left eye and his jugular vein by millimeters. He received several stitches and some pain medication, but miraculously he was released just a few hours later. Though he was deeply cut and bruised, we were spared a tragedy that day.

*It was a wakeup call.* Afterward we realized that there are no guarantees, and we looked at what we were doing as parents to love and train our children. We had been concerned about the physical state of our son. After all, he was severely injured and could have died that day. And yet, while every parent would respond like this if their child was in *physical* danger, we realized how easy it was to forget about the *spiritual* dangers facing our children.

Knowing our tendency to minimize or neglect the serious consequences of our spiritual rebellion and sin against God, Jesus made a profound statement emphasizing the precedence of the spiritual life over the physical life. He was sending out his disciples on one of their first mission trips, and before they left, he encouraged them with these words: "Do not fear those who kill the body but cannot kill the soul. Rather fear him who can destroy both soul and body in hell" (Matt. 10:28 ESV). Here Jesus gives us a key principle we need to remember as parents: *The death of a child's soul is far more important than the death of their body.*

When young people leave home today, they often leave the church behind as well. This is a symptom of a spiritual problem. Though their bodies are fine, their souls are not. In his book *You Lost Me,* author and researcher David Kinnaman says this about young people and the church: "Overall, there is a 43 percent drop-off between the teen and early adult years in terms of church engagement. These numbers represent about eight million twenty-somethings who were active churchgoers as teenagers but who will no longer be particularly engaged in a church by their thirtieth birthday."[1]

These eight million young adults were once active in church. And while the church certainly plays a role in the discipleship of children and teens, at the core this is not a *church* problem; it's a parenting problem. This large percentage of teenagers leaving the church when they leave home is a wakeup call to parents.

## SHOW THE SHEMA

When we think about our children in light of eternity, how does that change our priorities? What does spiritual parenting look like, given the serious consequences of a child rejecting Jesus? Of the 1,189 chapters in the Bible, Deuteronomy 6 stands out as one of the most helpful chapters we can turn to as a guide for spiritual parenting. It is an ancient creed that God gave to the nation of Israel, words intended to be recited and memorized. The Jews called it the *shema*, which is Hebrew for "hear," "listen," and "obey." Deuteronomy 6 is a command—God is telling his people to listen to him and obey what he is saying to them. Every day, as they were getting up and again as they were going to bed, observant Jews living at the time of Jesus would recite the *shema*. Even today it is often the first "prayer" that Jewish children are taught to say.[2]

> Hear, O Israel: The LORD our God, the LORD is one. You shall love the LORD your God with all your heart and with all your soul and with all your might. And these words that I command you today shall be on your heart. You shall teach them diligently to your children, and shall talk of them when you sit in your house, and when you walk by the way, and when you lie down, and when you rise. You shall bind them as a sign on your hand, and they shall be as frontlets between your eyes. You shall write them on the doorposts of your house and on your gates.
>
> —Deuteronomy 6:4–9 ESV

This passage shows us that God intends for parents to be discipling their children, and doing this through the everyday activities of life. This reveals the beauty and simplicity of God's methods, that he designed our relationships in the family in such a way that we can incorporate spiritual parenting into the natural flows and rhythms of life. Discipleship begins at home. And while it takes intentionality, putting these principles into practice isn't difficult. Let's take a closer look at what this passage in Deuteronomy teaches us about spiritual parenting.

*1. Talk about the Lord at home.* "You shall teach them diligently to your children, and shall talk of them when you sit in *your house*" (Deut. 6:7 ESV, emphasis added).

First of all, we learn that we should teach our children in our homes. The Hebrew verb for "teach them diligently" is *shanan*. In this context, it means teaching children repeatedly, not just once or twice.[3] So we should be repeatedly talking about the Lord throughout our day. While praying at meals and holding family devotions are great, this can also be done naturally as you have conversations throughout the day. *Shema*-style parenting means that you prioritize spending time together at home. This might mean saying no to outside commitments and activities so that you have extended moments together in the home. It might involve planning family time together and taking time to read the Bible with each of your children individually.

*2. Talk about the Lord along the road.* "And when you walk by *the way*" (Deut. 6:7 ESV, emphasis added).

For many parents in America, this passage is where much of their time with their kids is spent. In biblical times, people spent large portions of the day walking from place to place. The story we referenced earlier about Jesus walking twenty-five miles with his disciples is a great example. Today we spend this time in the car, driving. Let's not waste these hours! Driving along the road can allow for many practical opportunities for discipleship. Children may even find it easier to focus, and you can have conversations about school, their friendships, and even struggles they are facing. The car is often neutral territory. Sometimes it's easier to have a natural conversation with a child when you are driving home from sports practice rather than sitting at the dinner table.

Our children grow up quickly and head to college, the workforce, or the mission field, so take every opportunity to teach them as they grow. You may need to turn off the DVD player or the game system. Turn down the radio and remove some of the distractions to allow for conversation.

*3. Talk about the Lord when you go to bed and get up.* "And when you *lie down*, and when you *rise*" (Deut. 6:7 ESV, emphasis added).

Bedtime and mornings are natural rhythms that we all experience. These can also be some of the best times to pray and read from the Bible with your children, especially when they're young. As your kids get older, you may also want to focus on memorizing Scripture together. In high school, schedules often become more complicated—especially in the evenings—so many families schedule short devotional times in the morning before school.

CHAD: I love art — whether it's music, visual arts, or poetry — so spiritual paintings are very meaningful to me. Growing up, I remember a painting we had in our house depicting the return of the Prodigal Son from Luke 15. In this painting, the son wore modern-day clothes as he knelt on the ground with his father's arms around him. It was a beautiful painting representing God's love for his children, even when they've run away in sin and returned home.

The painting was always hanging on the wall, but one day my dad took it down to explain God's love to me and my sister. He explained the story and told us that no matter what we might do, he would always love and accept us as his children. Even if we did the worst thing imaginable, he would be there to embrace us. That painting is etched in my mind, and the lesson remains in my heart. Hanging that painting in our house was a way of putting God's Word on the "doorpost" of our home.

While this means getting up a little earlier for a brief reading, reflection, and prayer, it is a great way to start the day together as a family. Of course, nighttime also works well for connecting with your kids. One of my (Chad) best memories is of my mom tucking me into bed each night when I was a kid. What stands out most in my memory is how, after tucking me in, my mom would ask me my "pit and peak" of the day. This was our way of talking about the worst (pit) and the best (peak) moments of my day. She would share her pit and peak too, and we would pray together before I went to sleep. This gave us a daily connection time that remains sweet in my memory to this day.

4. *Use your hands, head, and house to talk about the Lord.* "You shall bind them as a sign on *your hand*, and they shall be as frontlets between *your eyes*. You shall write them on the doorposts of *your house* and on your gates" (Deut. 6:8–9 ESV, emphasis added).

The ancient Israelites made tiny boxes called "phylacteries," which involved writing Scripture on slips of paper and placing them inside these boxes and then tying them to their wrists, to the turbans wrapped around their heads, and to the doorframes of their houses. We're not advocating these Jewish practices, but we can all learn from the principle behind them—the need to emphasize the Word of God in our homes and in our daily lives. This passage simply illustrates that God's Word needs to be near us, a regular part of all we do. Perhaps this means actually framing a Scripture or hanging spiritual paintings around your house. Use every opportunity available to you to explore, apply, and discuss Scripture with your children.

# MAKING NECESSARY SACRIFICES

If you were to ask people in pastoral ministry what the biggest barrier to effective discipleship is today, they would likely say that people are just too busy. They don't have time to step away from the demands of life to focus on reading the Bible, praying, spending time with other believers. But the *shema*, as we have seen, isn't about stepping out of our busy lives to engage in a special program; it is about making the best use of the time we have for discipleship.

Still, there will be some sacrifices we need to make. We need to reset our schedules, looking for opportunities to disciple our children and remaining alert and responsive to God's Spirit. We (Jason, Bobby, and Chad) understand this because it has been a struggle in our own lives. There is always one more meeting or activity to attend. Often the church, with its programs and classes and activities, is part of the problem, and for a season, you may need to say no to specific opportunities to involve yourself in the church. Even though two of us (Bobby and Jason) are in pastoral ministry, parenting in the home is still our primary responsibility.

Ministry, like any commitment, can threaten precious family time, though the two don't always need to be in tension with one another.

Our family (Jason) has had to learn many of these lessons the hard way. As I began traveling more often with the Seeds Family Worship ministry, I realized that I wasn't always staying connected with my wife or kids. The Lord showed me that my call to minister to families was for *our family*, not just other families. I know this seems painfully obvious, but it wasn't easy to change my patterns and habits. As a family, we had to work through this with tears and some heavy conversations. Now we've made the adjustment to my travel and approach the ministry as a family commitment, not just something I do, which is far better for all of us. The Lord has blessed us with so many great memories as we have served him together in different ways. While it is easier for me (and less expensive) to travel and serve alone, ministering together allows me to keep my family first.

Speaking from the perspective of a pastor's kid (PK), I (Chad) can say something that isn't always true of most PKs. My dad was committed to his ministry and yet was still there for me when I needed him. Not until I was older did I realize what a challenge this is for parents, balancing their ministry (whether full-time or volunteer) with their family life. Over and over again, I have heard of pastors' sons and daughters who felt neglected because their parents were so involved ministering to other people. My dad came home at the end of each day, and we spent a lot of time together. We had dinner together practically every night. These simple priorities go a long way toward communicating love and making sure your children know they are valued and important.

Our culture values being busy. We increasingly work longer hours, and employers expect their employees to always be available through phone calls and email. More and more today, we see parents who neglect relationships with their children for work.

It might be checking an email during dinner or taking a phone call at a soccer game, but the result is the same: our children do not get our undivided attention. Children need parents who are dedicated to giving them the gift of their presence. Kids may not immediately realize what you're giving them, but speaking from experience, we can tell you that it will have a profound impact on their spiritual development. The truth is that parents *must* sacrifice some of their personal wants and desires for their kids. Too many of us are doing too many unimportant things; we need to focus on what matters most. Reverse these trends by walking the narrow path of discipleship.

Here's a significant truth that I (Jason) have learned through my own struggles as a father trying to find balance in the busyness of life. Sometimes as parents we need to decide, in advance, to "save the best for last." What do I mean by this? When our children were young, I found that at the end of a long day at work, I was physically and emotionally exhausted. I gave away all of my best energy and emotion trying to run our small business. So by the time I got home, I was *spent*. More honestly, I was looking for a place to hide out and recharge. But I saw that my family needed me. I came to realize that I had to plan and save energy so that I had something left to invest into my wife and children.

Following this realization, I learned the importance of *scheduling time* with my family. I began putting dates on my calendar to reserve time together. This was a breakthrough for me (and for us), because I struggle to say no to good things. I get caught up in the moment without considering all of the costs, and then my family ends up paying the price. With family time scheduled, I know that every Monday and Tuesday night, I'm committed to eating dinner with my wife and kids. It is written in my weekly schedule. If I am asked to do something on one of those nights, I say I have plans, and I don't feel any obligation to explain myself. Commit to spend time with your family, and then write it down. You won't regret it!

All of this will involve making sacrifices. Andy Stanley writes about a common issue that families face today: we're all "cheaters." In his book *Choosing to Cheat*, he describes how everyone cheats something in their life—their hobbies, their job, or their family, for example. We should choose what we will cheat.[4] The truth we must face is that there are not enough resources available to us to do everything we can possibly do in our busy North American culture. Every area of life vies for our attention, but we have only so much time in the day. Why is this important to understand? Because we often think that the problem is time management— finding more time to get everything done. The real problem isn't fitting more into our busy day; it's setting priorities. *What will you choose to cheat?* Whatever you do, you will end up cheating something or someone, so make sure it's an intentional choice that truly aligns with your priorities in life.

## THE UPS AND DOWNS

The *shema* is important not only in the regular rhythms of your family's daily schedule but also in the midst of life's difficulties— those times when your child is hurt, broken, and vulnerable. Your son didn't make the soccer team, your daughter's friends abandoned her on a Friday night, or one of your kids failed to make the marching band. These are the inevitable struggles and pains of life in this world. Every child experiences them, and you cannot protect your children from this disappointment and pain. Nor should you.

When your children are struggling, you have an opportunity to tenderly love them. That's why it's important to be there for your child when they are suffering and asking questions about life. This is equally true during the good times, the times of celebrating and rejoicing with them. All of this is vital for proper spiritual nurturing, because in these moments, you help your children learn to trust God. Over time, the day-to-day experiences of life's joys and disappointments add up, and children develop a mature understanding of how to live in relationship with God, regardless of life's circumstances.

Times of sadness, doubt, and hurt are a normal part of growing up, and parents have an opportunity to disciple their kids as they wrestle through them. These times will shape children for better or for worse, and what parents choose to do (or not to do) can make a world of difference.

I (Chad) remember struggling with my faith as I started high school. In ninth grade, I experienced a great deal of anxiety and depression, and my parents noticed. These emotions were new for me; I was generally a happy kid growing up. But as the social pressures of high school got to me, my middle school days of getting along with everyone and fitting in ended. As I sank into depression, I entered an intense season of spiritual doubt.

We had a side room in the house dedicated to our computer and TV. I remember coming home from school one day, feeling sad and anxious. I turned on the computer in the back of the room and searched for "signs of depression" on the internet. I was reading about the symptoms when it finally hit me: *I am depressed.*

I realized that I had been in denial about my depression. I had tried to hide it, but my dad saw my struggle. I remember a time when he was driving me to football practice and he asked me how I was. I did my best to mask my sadness. I was embarrassed. Though I was reading my Bible and telling others about my faith, I had few friends who shared my faith commitment. Mostly, I felt alone.

Driving with my dad, I burst into tears.

My father listened as I poured out my heart to him. I shared my struggles with being a Christian in a public school, surrounded by people who didn't follow Christ. Talking through my difficulties that day with my dad helped me unload some of the burden I was feeling. Looking back, my parents' support really helped me stay committed to Christ in high school.

BOBBY: The hardest thing a parent ever goes through is watching your child struggle. When they struggle, you struggle with them, and you often feel helpless. The most important thing in these times is to let your children know that you love them. Instruction, discipline, and general guidance are good, but they need to be rooted in a relationship of love. Love is the foundation. If your children know you love them, they will feel free to open up to you and share their hearts, their fears, and their struggles. When my son, Chad, struggled with anxiety in high school, I didn't always know what to say to him, but I knew he needed to know how much I loved him and how much I believed that God would help him.

That day on the way to football practice wasn't an isolated incident. I recall many nights when I stayed up late sitting on the couch in the middle of the computer room asking my dad questions about faith, God, and the Bible—very difficult but honest questions—and he took the time to listen and respond and pray over me. I'll never forget his love and grace during this time, as he walked with me through one of the most challenging seasons of my life.

My mom and dad were always intentional about our relationship, and over the next few years there were other times when I was able to open up and admit my deep-rooted struggles of anxiety and depression. My parents were able to guide me in ways that shaped me into the man I have become. Today, though I still struggle at times, I know how to deal with the bondage of anxiety and depression. Praise God!

# DEDICATION IN ACTION

REMEMBER. Memorize Deuteronomy 6:4–7 as a family.

> Hear, O Israel: The LORD our God, the LORD is one. You shall love the LORD your God with all your heart and with all your soul and with all your might. And these words that I command you today shall be on your heart. You shall teach them diligently to your children, and shall talk of them when you sit in your house, and when you walk by the way, and when you lie down, and when you rise. (ESV)

CONSIDER. Write down ideas of how you can disciple your children in each of the following areas.

- As you sit in your house
- As you walk (or drive) along the way
- As you lie down
- As you get up

PRAY. Ask the Lord to reveal to you specific areas where your children may be struggling. Pray for the ability to speak the truth into their lives, directed by the Holy Spirit.

RESPOND. How is the Holy Spirit leading you *today* to live out your dedication to God in spiritual parenting?

LISTEN. "Impress Them" (Deut. 6:4–7), *The Word of God*, Seeds Family Worship.

# CHAPTER 4

# DEDICATED TO JESUS

YOUR RELATIONSHIP WITH JESUS is the most important thing you bring to the table as a parent. Without it, everything else you attempt will fall short of God's best for your family. Dedication always has a goal. When Christian parents dedicate their child, they are dedicating him or her to a person—Jesus Christ. We are dedicating ourselves to serving Jesus, raising our precious, God-given child to know Jesus, to follow him, and to obey his teachings. It is hard to dedicate our children to Jesus without personally knowing him ourselves because we will grow frustrated at our constant mistakes and failures. We will lack the power necessary to raise children for Christ in the world today. In the same way, if we go through the motions of attending church, reading the Bible, and praying the Lord's Prayer without having a relationship with him, we will just have empty religion. We will pass along religious behaviors without really introducing our kids to the person of Jesus. And if we know only *the cross* of Jesus—as important as that is—we will miss out on his life and his Spirit in us. Every other object of our dedication—worship, word, prayer, the church, and the kingdom—depends on knowing the person of Jesus.

Jesus is the center of our faith. He is the one we trust and follow. The apostle Paul is an example of a leader dedicated to Jesus. He wrote, "I have been crucified with Christ. It is no longer I who live, but Christ who lives in me" (Gal. 2:20 ESV). If we disciple our kids but leave out the active presence of the living Christ in our lives, our labor is in vain. We must first model for them the person we want them to be. As the saying goes, "You can't teach what you don't know, and you can't lead where you won't go." Being a disciple who trusts and follows Jesus must be more than just something we talk about; it is something we are. We must personally embrace Christ before we can make followers of Christ. In fact, the degree to which spiritual parents know Christ largely determines the degree to which they will influence their children to know him.

## ARE YOU TRULY DEDICATED TO JESUS?

The type of relationship with God we are talking about is not just a transaction in which we check off the "saved" box on the ballot of life, making Jesus our Savior.[1] Being dedicated to Jesus means that we come back to Jesus day in and day out, relating to him as our Savior and King (Lord). He's the number one priority on which we center our lives. That includes parenting. Even though parenting our children is vital, knowing and following Jesus is more important. He needs to be our first love.

If we are leading our families toward Christ and calling it *discipleship*, we must remember that it is Christ whom we are following, not just an assortment of religious teachings and practices. As Dietrich Bonhoeffer once said, "Christianity without the living Christ is inevitably Christianity without discipleship, and Christianity without discipleship is always Christianity without Christ."[2] We make disciples of Jesus so they follow him. We are not merely passing on Christianity or a set of moral teachings. We give our children more than an encouragement to have faith; we give them Jesus. Through the gospel and the work of the Holy Spirit, we want to introduce them to the living Christ.

The night before Jesus died, he gave his disciples one of the keys to eternal life. He poured out his soul to God and remembered the friends and followers he would soon leave behind. He said that he was giving them eternal life, and then he defined what that means: "This is eternal life, that they know you the only true God, and Jesus Christ whom you have sent" (John 17:3 ESV). Jesus said that his Father had given him authority to give eternal life to whomever he wished, and he defined that life as *knowing God and himself.* Jesus tells us that in him we find the life we've always longed for, and he says that he gives us this life in lavish proportions (John 10:10).

Imagine that we are sitting together, enjoying some quiet time, talking about our hopes, dreams, and desires, and I ask this question: "Where is *your* heart? What's your dream for your kids?" If your desire is that your children follow Jesus, be honest with where you are in your relationship with him as well. That's where the dedication journey begins.

# ABOVE THE NOISE

Our lives are filled with senseless noise that constantly distracts us from the things that matter most. We want to invite you to pause right now to think about your relationship with Jesus. Take a moment to read the following song lyrics, and as you read, pray for the Lord to speak to you about where your relationship with him is.

### ABOVE THE NOISE
Lately I've been restless, my heart has been consumed
With everything, everything but you
Lately I've been foolish; I've given my life to
Everything, everything but you
When you're all I really need
And you call me to greater things

Above the noise
Far from the crowd
Quiet the voices that are trying to drown out
Your Holy Word, Your Sacred Truth
Help me to lift my eyes, and lift my heart to you
Above the noise

Right here in this moment, right here in this room
I don't need anything, anything but you
Right here in your presence, my eyes are set on you
I don't need anything, anything but you
'Cause you're all I really need
And you call me to greater things

Above the noise
Far from the crowd
Quiet the voices that are trying to drown out
Your Holy Word, Your Sacred Truth
Help me to lift my eyes, and lift my heart to you
Above the noise

*—Jason Ingram and Jason Houser*

Take a deep breath and close your eyes. Be still for a moment before you read on. We encourage you to pray the following prayer as we take this next step together:

*Jesus, my desire is to seek you right now. Protect me from lies and help me to hear only your voice. I need you to fill me with your truth. I pray that your Spirit will give me honest insight into the condition of my heart so I can see my current relationship with you. In Jesus' name, amen.*

You may feel tempted to move past this moment and press forward, but please slow down. Wait on the Lord. It is critical to examine the foundation of our hearts before we seek to build our family. Jesus calls us to fully surrender our lives to him. He deserves to be the Lord (master) of our lives. We often tell people that Jesus does not want to be a *part* of your life. He wants to *be* your life. For this reason, we need the gospel. The gospel is the key that unlocks the door to relationship with Jesus.

## THE STORYLINE OF THE GOSPEL

The word *gospel* simply means "good news." The death, burial, and resurrection of Jesus is the heart of the gospel, but these events make sense only within a larger storyline that begins in Genesis and runs through the entire Bible. Jesus is the gospel; he is the good news we need to hear (Mark 1:1; Luke 2:8–11). He is the Messiah, the long promised King of Israel and the world. In Jesus, we find forgiveness of our sins against God, we find direction for our lives, and we begin to grasp God's purposes for this world and his kingdom. The person of Jesus fits within the broader story of God's relationship with humanity. Maybe you've heard this before, but if you haven't, let's review some of the key movements in the story.[3]

- *Creation and the fall.* God is holy and loving. He created us for himself in the Garden of Eden. We rebelled against God. We are all now separated from him, gravitating to sin in thought, word, and deed, yet God is gracious. He chose a man named Abraham and promised to bless the world through him. Abraham believed God and became the father of the nation of Israel and carried on the promises of God.

- *Redemption.* God sent Jesus into the world to establish his kingdom as King and Savior. Jesus is the fulfillment of all God's promises, starting with the promise of blessing to Abraham. He took the penalty for our sin by dying in our place on the cross, receiving the punishment we deserved. Three days later he rose from the dead and conquered death. He defeated Satan and now gives us new life through the gift of the Holy

Spirit. Jesus is the Way, and through faith in him—in his sacrifice and resurrection—we are brought into a right relationship with God and enter his kingdom. Jesus has ascended to heaven, where he reigns until his return. He redeems people—those who respond to him by turning from their sin and trusting and following him as they rely on his power.

- *Restoration.* One day soon Jesus will return for us, when he comes back to judge the living and the dead. At that time, his reign will be fully established. He will take his children into the eternal kingdom in the newly established paradise of God in the new heaven and new earth.

The gospel is a rich and wonderful story, and we've touched on only the high points here. It's the story of Jesus, and it's good news because all of God's promises for humanity are fulfilled in him. When we place our faith in Jesus, trusting him to lead our lives and to be our King and master, we are adopted into God's family, and the promises of God become ours.

# THE HEART OF THE GOSPEL

Within the larger gospel narrative that flows from Genesis to Revelation, there is a core message that communicates how we go from being blinded, sinful rebels against God to being accepted and loved by him. We get to join his kingdom now and in eternity. Trapped as slaves to our sin, dead to God and deaf to his Word, we must be *saved* from our sin and its consequences. The Bible tells us that our eternal destiny depends on whether we are saved by God through Jesus. These words in 1 Corinthians 15:1–6 describe the heart of the gospel: "Now I would remind you, brothers, of the gospel I preached to you, which you received, in which you stand, and by which you are being saved, if you hold fast to the word I preached to you—unless you believed in vain. For I delivered to you as of first importance what I also received ..." (ESV).

Paul's language will make one thing clear—faith in Jesus and in his death, burial, and resurrection is at the heart of the gospel, and it determines the basis of your standing with God. You are saved by what Jesus has done through your faith in him. There is nothing more important than this! This passage goes on to summarize the core gospel message: "For I delivered to you as of first importance what I also received: that Christ died for our sins in accordance with the Scriptures, that he was buried, that he was raised on the third day in accordance with the Scriptures, and that he appeared to Cephas, then to the twelve. Then he appeared to more than five hundred brothers at one time, most of whom are still alive, though some have fallen asleep" (ESV).

Here, the focus of the gospel is on Jesus Christ's death, burial, and resurrection *and how they make sense in accordance with the broader story of Scripture*. The first part of this summary is that Christ died for our sins. Jesus is God's Son, and he conquered sin, Satan, and death. He is now the reigning King of humanity, and his kingdom will be fully consummated when he returns.

The historical reality of Jesus and his death, burial, resurrection, and ascension leads us to three key truths.

1. God is holy and loving. He created us for himself, but we have rebelled against him by self-rule and sin.
2. God sent Jesus to save us from self-rule and sin through his life, death, and resurrection.
3. God forgives and receives into his kingdom people who repent and dedicate their lives to Jesus through faith.

Being "saved" is not something we do. It's not something we work to achieve. It's something God does for us and in us. That's what the Bible means when it says we are saved by grace. Grace means it is a free gift. God saves us, not because we deserve it but because we place our trust in what he says and what he does for us, on our behalf. This is what the Bible means when it states, "By grace you have been saved through faith. And this is not your own doing; it is the gift of God" (Eph. 2:8 ESV).[4] John 3:16 tells us that what God has done for us in Jesus is an expression of his love for us: "God so loved the world, that he gave his only Son, that whoever believes in him should not perish but have eternal life" (ESV).

This is far more than just a transaction in which God pays our fine and we receive a free pass on punishment for our sin. It's a change in our status, in our relationship, and the way we live. We move from the kingdom of darkness into Jesus' kingdom (Col. 1:13). We enter into a life of trusting and following Jesus. Jesus describes it as being adopted into a new family, being connected organically to a growing vine and bearing fruit as we draw life from the vine (John 15:1–4). The Bible tells us that we now relate to one another as part of a single "body," the body of Jesus Christ. The apostle Paul says, "You are not your own, for you were bought with a price. So glorify God in your body" (1 Cor. 6:19–20 ESV). Jesus takes away our sins and transforms our lives so that we can now live under his kingship.

# DEDICATING YOURSELF TO JESUS

Covenants are a big deal in the Bible. A covenant is a special relationship in which parties formally commit themselves to each other. It is an agreement in which God freely binds and commits himself to human beings, and human beings respond in turn and commit themselves to God. You enter into a covenant with God when you make the decision to trust and follow Jesus (become a disciple).

The Israelites had a special covenant relationship with God, in which he made them into a nation and gave them a special place in history. God now commits himself to everyone who comes to him through Jesus in a covenant of faith. He promises that we receive forgiveness of all sins, the indwelling presence of his Holy Spirit, life in his kingdom, and eternal life in heaven. We enter into this "new covenant" by turning from self-rule and sin, confessing with our mouths our faith in Jesus, and then sealing our faith commitment through baptism.

I (Bobby) have performed many wedding ceremonies, which are a celebration and declaration of a covenant between a man and a woman. According to tradition, the pastor asks the man if he will take the woman to be his wife, promising before God, his family, and his friends that he will stay with her in sickness and in health, in prosperity and in adversity, so long as they both shall live. Then the pastor turns and asks the woman the same thing. These vows they make in the marriage ceremony are the basis of their covenant, an agreement between the two parties, in which they pledge themselves to each other. Covenants, like a wedding ceremony, involve commitment, confession, and physical expression.

The wedding ceremony is one of the best analogies for describing how you become dedicated to Jesus, because just like in a marriage, dedication to Jesus is a lifelong commitment. Once you enter into the covenant relationship, your life will never be the same.

Do you want to place your faith in Jesus? We recommend that you find a Bible-believing church and ask for help in the following three areas.

1. *Commitment.* Make the decision to repent of your sins and turn to God through Jesus (Acts 26:20).
2. *Confession.* Confess your belief that Jesus is Lord — in all that he is and has done — and call on his name (Acts 22:16; 16:30–33).
3. *Physical Expression.* Be baptized as a covenant expression of the decision to trust and follow Jesus (Matt. 28:19–20; Acts 2:38).[5]

These three items are all closely tied together in the Bible as the way for people to dedicate themselves to Jesus in a covenant relationship. God is the one who draws us to himself, so that even the desire for this relationship starts long before we ever decide to follow him. When you respond to his invitation, God will come to live in you through his Holy Spirit. The Bible describes it this way: "Now you Gentiles have also heard the truth, the Good News that God saves you. And when you believed in Christ, he identified you as his own by giving you the Holy Spirit, whom he promised long ago" (Eph. 1:13 NLT).

Remember, God provides us with this covenant — the gift of his indwelling Spirit, the forgiveness of sins, and a new life — and it is all by grace (a free gift). Our response is faith. Faith means we truly trust and follow Jesus. Such faith will lead you into a life of discipleship. This is the greatest decision you will ever make, the fundamental first step for all parents who want to disciple their children. Those who have made this decision are those who are "in Christ" (Rom. 6:3). Once we are in Christ, our whole approach to the family changes. We move from being parents who operate on a foundation of wordly wisdom to being parents who operate from our identity in Christ. Your relationship with Jesus is the single most important thing for your life. And it is the best gift you can give to your children as a parent. We urge you to make this commitment today. Jesus makes us right with God. And Jesus is the Way, the Truth, and the Life that our families need.

# DEDICATION IN ACTION

REMEMBER. Memorize John 3:16–18 as a family.

God so loved the world, that he gave his only Son, that whoever believes in him should not perish but have eternal life. For God did not send his Son into the world to condemn the world, but in order that the world might be saved through him. Whoever believes in him is not condemned, but whoever does not believe is condemned already, because he has not believed in the name of the only Son of God. (ESV)

CONSIDER. Have you received God's grace and dedicated yourself to Jesus? This is a radical change in your life, and how you answer this question will have a major impact on your parenting.

PRAY. Ask God to help you take the next step in your relationship with Christ.

RESPOND. How is the Holy Spirit leading you *today* to be dedicated to Jesus?

LISTEN. "Eternal Life" (John 3:16), *Seeds of Faith*, Seeds Family Worship.

# CHAPTER 5

# DEDICATED TO FAMILY WORSHIP

IN THE PREVIOUS CHAPTER, we saw that being a dedicated parent, training your child to trust and follow Jesus, requires that you personally focus on Jesus in a way that transforms every aspect of who you are. God is raising your children, and he uses you to do it! Being a parent is an honor and a responsibility, but it will demand everything you have to faithfully disciple children.

So what does spiritual formation look like in the trenches, in the day-to-day experiences of family life? In this chapter, we want to offer a framework for what we refer to as "family worship." There are many different ways to think about family worship, and in this section, we want to present several ideas and options out of which you can discern the best way for your family to love God together, all in a way that is unique to you and your context. We will give examples of how to bring this framework to life, by sketching out what our families and friends have done. And while this will give you some ideas, you will want to seek the Lord's guidance as you apply this to your own personality and family dynamics.

That said, what we're advocating here is simply *a regular family time when you seek God together.* This doesn't require preparing a sermon or playing a guitar to lead singing, though for some families it might involve just that. It does mean that you, the parent, must work to create an atmosphere that helps your family worship God. This can take many forms, as we will see, but there are several common elements.

A regular time for family worship will likely be challenging, stretching, and awkward for you (and your family) at first. Your kids or spouse may push back and be critical. We have seen in our own experience that there is a real spiritual battle that takes place. The enemy wants nothing more than to discourage you from discipling your children.

# FAMILY WORSHIP FINGERPRINT

The ministry that I (Jason) have been blessed to lead is called Seeds Family Worship, and we regularly get questions from parents who want to learn how to lead and engage their family in worship together. One of the couples who serve with the ministry, Philip and Jessica Morlan, have been used by God to help many parents get started on this journey. When they talk with parents, they encourage them to discover what they refer to as their "family worship fingerprint."

Consider how amazing it is that we each have different fingerprints. Every person is unique, one of a kind. This speaks to the creativity, power, and precision of our God. Philip and Jessica have found that, just as every person has their own individual fingerprint, each family has their own distinct personality. And that comes through in the way you and your family engage in worship. Your family worship fingerprint is unique to your family. It is determined by the size of your family, the age of your children, the place and time you choose for worship, as well as the personality, character, and gifts of each family member.

Why is this important to understand? Because we want you to feel the freedom to be creative and flexible. Some parents get locked into feeling as if they need to copy what others are doing, or they feel pressure to implement routines and practices that are unnatural and don't really fit their family. We want you to grasp that *family worship is going to look different in each of our homes.* And that's how it should be. This is part of God's grand design.

God has made every family unique, and every family has its own strengths and weaknesses. Each family will see its share of blessings and challenges. We all have gifts the Lord has given each of us for a specific purpose—to show his greatness and do good works (Eph. 2:10). And yet, at the same time, we are all dysfunctional in different ways because we live in a fallen world, impacted by sin. The Lord uses the closeness of our family relationships to challenge us and change us so that we become more like him. We refer to this as the process of *sanctification*—growing in holiness to become more and more like Jesus.

Your family's challenges may include raising children in a single-parent home or having a blended family. Some of you may be in a home where both parents work full-time (and are struggling to make ends meet) or where one parent is constantly required to travel out of town for a job. There may be health issues with either parent or with the child. You are not alone; every family has its own struggles, and they weigh heavily on our hearts in different ways.

At the same time, every family has a river of unique blessings from the Lord. Our children themselves are one of these blessings. As it says in Psalm 127:3, "Children are a heritage from the LORD, the fruit of the womb a reward" (ESV). Your family may have other blessings as well, like a strong church family, a godly heritage and wonderful grandparents, or a good, stable job.

Each family needs to seek God to help them discover how to disciple their children well. As we learned from Deuteronomy 6 (see chap. 3 of this book), the Bible instructs us to teach our kids as we move through our lives—as we wake up, as we go to bed, as we venture through our day, and as we rest at home. We want to dig even deeper to help you apply a couple of these principles from Deuteronomy 6 to family worship. Our personal examples are written to give you ideas on how you may want to structure your family worship time.

## As You Lie Down

First, you can seek the Lord together as you "lie down." My family (Jason) has a rhythm, which I influence, that determines how we flow through our week. We have less structure than some families in how we approach our time together. At the same time, my wife and I are committed to discipling our children consistently. We accomplish this by sitting down with our kids in our living room right before or after they get ready for bed, several times a week. We started doing this when our children were very young, reading them Bible stories from resources like *The Beginner's Bible*. We graduated to other paraphrased Bibles and devotionals.[1] We also loved *The Jesus Storybook Bible* when our kids were younger.

Now that our children are older, we use different resources, or we just read through a book of the Bible and talk about how to apply it to our lives. We have read an anime (short for Japanese animations) series called the *Power Bible: Bible Stories to Impart Wisdom*. Our kids connect with the pictures, and we like how the images inspire different conversations. We also love Phil Vischer's DVD series called *What's in the Bible?* This series gives families a good grasp of the entire biblical narrative. The DVDs are incredibly educational and a whole lot of fun to watch as a family.

As we begin any family worship time, we start with a brief prayer and then seek to learn from the Bible. We use resources (like those mentioned above) to study, and then we always talk about how what we read applies to our lives. Finally, we close in prayer.

## When You Rise

Philip and Jessica Morlan, whom I mentioned earlier, have five children, and all of them have busy schedules and are involved in many different activities outside the home. Philip and Jessica knew they wanted to make family worship a priority, so after much prayer and discussion, they realized that the only time they could consistently do this well was early in the morning.

They chose to have everyone meet for breakfast at 6:20 a.m. every school day. This works well for them because the children's school schedule is fixed, and it establishes the routine for their family. The family was already gathering to eat breakfast in the morning, so they simply decided to be intentional. Now they are being fed physically *and* spiritually at the same time. Philip starts out the time by praying, and then he leads a devotion and discussion for about fifteen to twenty minutes. The family is currently reading through Sally Michael's book *God's Providence*, which is a resource connected to John Piper's ministry, Children Desiring God *(www.childrendesiringGod.org)*. They have also found it valuable to choose specific passages in the Bible that relate to things happening in their home. Often they will use the book of Proverbs to speak into any challenges they may be dealing with as a family.

I have had the privilege of staying in their home and have participated in their morning devotions. After waking up and heading to the kitchen table, I wondered whether the clanking of spoons and bowls and the passing of food around the table would distract the kids from connecting with the day's lesson. I was surprised to find that the activity at the table actually helped the children stay engaged. Larger families can often benefit from a more structured and scheduled approach like this.

◆　◆　◆

These are just two families, two examples of how to engage in family worship. Keep in mind that neither the Housers' nor the Morlans' method of family worship is inherently right or wrong; they are just different. Both families are seeking God, as described in Deuteronomy 6, in their own way.

BOBBY: Our children are now older, but when they were younger, we had family worship at suppertime and near bedtime. After supper each evening, we would pull out a children's Bible storybook or devotional for two or three minutes to read a story. Then we would talk for another minute or two about what the story meant, keeping it at their level of understanding. We ended with a brief prayer. The whole experience took no more than five minutes. Sometimes we would listen to a song and try to sing along and then read through one verse of the song. It was always simple, but the key thing wasn't what we did; it was the regularity and consistency — day to day, week to week. My advice for parents of small children: make it short. Remember, "faith comes from hearing, and hearing through the word of Christ" (Rom. 10:17 ESV). A child's mind wanders, because attention spans are limited. The goal is to form habits and practices, teaching kids the importance of getting into the Word briefly every day.

When our children became teenagers, we found that the best time to do devotions was now early in the morning. But we still kept it simple: each of us would take a turn reading a short passage or a devotional thought. Again, the key was doing it regularly.

People have asked, "Were there times when they didn't pay attention?"

Yes.

"As teenagers, did they push back on the practice?"

Sometimes.

But we stuck to it, and it was just part of what our family did.

Voddie Bauckham, in his book *Family Driven Faith*, offers seven values of family worship. They can give you some principles to think through as you consider what might work best for your family.[2]

1. Having a time of worship must be born of conviction.
2. It begins with the head of the household.
3. It must be scheduled.
4. It must be simple.
5. It must be natural.
6. It must be mandatory.
7. It must be participatory.

While we think all of these are helpful, you may want to emphasize some of them more than others. Again, family worship is unique to each family.

# BIBLICAL EXAMPLES OF WORSHIP

Biblical writers frequently describe worship in ways that reflect action, as something that involves our bodies and not just our minds. Family worship certainly starts with the heart; it must be born of genuine love and affection for the Lord. In ancient Israel, there were many times when the people of God could not contain their emotions in their worship of God. After winning a battle, they would break out in song and dance. If they knew they needed to repent of sin, they tore their clothes, mourning as an act of worship. When they experienced the presence of God, they fell on their faces. These practices are scattered throughout Scripture. The people's worship flowed outward from the heart through actions.

One of the most vivid examples of this in the Bible is David's delightful dance as the people brought the ark of the covenant to Jerusalem. The people of Israel ushered in the ark with shouting and the sound of the trumpet. So how did the king of Israel, who was a man after God's own heart, worship?

David danced before God with everything he had. His actions flowed naturally from his heart and were an expression of God's worth. Sadly, his wife thought he was disgraceful, not delightful. But God certainly didn't agree with her!

*Worship* is first and foremost a verb, which David's actions show. It is motivated by a desire to honor another. The Bible includes a wide range of physical movement and expression in its images of worship, including bowing down, lifting hands, clapping hands, dancing, holding processions, and singing.

"Worship," *Dictionary of Biblical Imagery* (Downers Grove, Ill.: Inter-Varsity Press, 1998), 970.

Worship is an expression and enactment of the greatest commandment — loving God with everything we have and everything we are. Worship can happen naturally and spontaneously, as we see in many places in Scripture, but we can also build structures into our lives for worship, especially as we consider family worship. Keep in mind that while worship often involves singing or the use of music, worship is more than singing a few songs. Everything we do in appreciation of the greatness of God qualifies as worship. Prayer, reading God's Word, speaking about his goodness, confessing our sin and our need for God's grace — all of these activities honor God and are expressions of worship. Even the way we go about our daily lives, the way we treat others, how we do our work — this can be worship as well.

When we talk about family worship, we aren't saying that this is the only way you worship God. It's simply a time when you gather as a family to worship God *together*. And this can be a powerful experience for your family. Once you decide you will worship together — expressing your love to God in regular practices — just watch and see what he will do!

Your experience might be like that of the Morlans, who saw a powerful transformation occur in their family shortly after they started meeting in the mornings. As a father, Philip was sensing some distance in his relationship with one of his daughters,

Maddy. She shared with him that she was feeling discouraged and didn't have time to do the personal daily devotions her small group at church was committed to doing. Philip saw her slowly drifting away from him and from the Lord, and he knew he needed to do something.

Philip sat down with his daughter and gave her a couple of options. He offered to get up an hour earlier in the morning and do the devotions with her. He also suggested that she consider doing the devotions with her younger sister before bedtime, to get help and encouragement from her. Philip was a bit surprised when Maddy came to him the next day and wanted to go with the first option. It meant getting up at 5:20 a.m.!

I don't know about you, but as a parent, giving up an extra hour of sleep in the morning is a real sacrifice, especially when

CHAD: I'm thankful for our family worship time when I was growing up. I enjoy structure, and I liked that we set aside a specific time for reading the Bible and praying together while I was in high school. Being a morning person, I also enjoyed the morning routine. I know it was a struggle for my dad — because he's not a morning person — but he did it anyway. It was a great example to me.

I still remember one morning in particular. We read Proverbs 3:7: "Do not be wise in your own eyes; fear the Lord and shun evil." The truth about humility stuck with me: "Do not be wise in your own eyes." When I went to my hockey game that night, I was still thinking about this verse. God used that morning reading to make me a better hockey player; instead of playing with pride, I tried to have a posture of humility on the ice. Experiences like that build up over time. God will use these times to shape your children in a way that affects their entire lives. His Word has amazing power to impact your family.

your family is already meeting at 6:20 a.m. for family worship at breakfast. But Philip knew that his relationship with his daughter was worth it. He followed through with the commitment and has found that the result has been greater than he could have hoped. Not only did he and his daughter begin to reconnect through these times together; his other children began to get up early — on their own — to have personal devotions. They observed their dad and oldest sister doing it and followed what they saw modeled for them. A dedicated father who was willing to make a sacrifice saw the blessing that ensued — not only for his relationship with his daughter but also for his entire family.

## GETTING STARTED WITH FAMILY WORSHIP

As we speak at various churches around the country, we have found that most parents did not have family worship when they were children. In other words, *most Christian families do not regularly practice family worship*. Again, we're not talking about church attendance or taking your kids to youth group (which are both good things). We are talking about time as a family when you worship God together, apart from programs and church events.

You might be surprised to learn that this used to be a common practice for Christian families. In the 1640s, Christian leaders in Scotland even held parents accountable for family worship. In the *Directory for Family Worship*, you can read what was expected of these parents: "The assembly requires and appoints ministers to make diligent search and inquiry, whether there be among them a family or families which neglect the duty of family worship. If such a family is found, the head of the family is to be admonished privately to amend his fault; and in case of his continuing therein, he is to be gravely and sadly reproved by the session; after which reproof, if he is found still to neglect family worship, let him be, for his obstinacy in such an offense, suspended and debarred from the Lord's supper, until the amen."[3]

If you didn't practice family worship, you weren't allowed to receive Communion. Our point is not to argue for church discipline on this matter, but we do think it is good to be reminded of our past and the priorities of Christians from previous generations. We can learn from what they did as we understand the importance they placed on family worship. It's also good to realize that family worship is not the latest fad. It is rooted in the ancient biblical command God gave to his people in Deuteronomy 6 and is something that has been practiced in every generation down through the ages.

If you aren't sure where to get started with family worship, we want to give you a simple and practical tool to help you begin incorporating family worship in your home. We've included a family worship devotion at the end of this chapter. Before we walk through the steps of this devotion, here's what you will need:

- A regular place to meet in your home
- A CD player, computer, or musical instrument(s)
- At least one Bible

This family devotional will get you started living out the principles we've been discussing in this book. It's a resource created in partnership with the family ministry leaders at Real Life Ministries in Post Falls, Idaho, for use by families in their church. And it's a tool that will help your family learn how to develop the following essential spiritual disciplines.

- Prayer
- Praising God
- Seeking him in his Word
- Applying his Word to your life as a family

This is not complicated. All you need to do is listen to a Scripture song together, pray a prayer that is written out for you, read several verses from the Bible as well as some background information on them, and then discuss what this means to you as a family.

Go ahead and take the next step. Find some time this evening or tomorrow morning to work through the devotion with your family. You can do this!

# STAND YOUR GROUND

As we mentioned at the beginning of this chapter, there is a battle going on right now for the hearts of your children. We see it in our culture, how the world wants to shape our children's worldview according to its rules and values. Our families have an enemy who wants to lead our children away from the Lord. There are two kingdoms in conflict: the kingdom of God and the kingdom of Satan. Conflicts between these two kingdoms will inevitably surface when you practice family worship.

In Ephesians 6:10–13, the apostle Paul reveals what is going on behind the scenes, and he encourages us to find our strength in the Lord: "Be strong in the Lord and in his mighty power. Put on the full armor of God, so that you can take your stand against the devil's schemes. For our struggle is not against flesh and blood, but against the rulers, against the authorities, against the powers of this dark world and against the spiritual forces of evil in the heavenly realms. Therefore put on the full armor of God, so that when the day of evil comes, you may be able to stand your ground, and after you have done everything, to stand."

Parents have told us many stories of the spiritual struggle that ensued when they decided to lead their families in worship in their homes. Be forewarned! This won't be easy. It is going to take determination on your part to trust God for strength as you press through these challenges. But take heart and know that you are standing your ground every time you teach your children from God's Word, every time you sing praise to God in your home, and every time you pray on behalf of your family. The battle belongs to the Lord, and our strength comes from him. Never forget the promise of Jesus: he is with you — always. So stand your ground!

I (Bobby) witnessed this spiritual battle firsthand. When I was growing up, I loved my dad, but because of his struggles with alcohol and his temper, my sisters and I were not sure about trusting him as a father. We were not a practicing Christian family, but my dad had a good heart and nominal Christian roots. One evening, just before supper, he asked us all as a family to be quiet because he was going to pray. In that moment, because I did not know about God and because of my feelings about my dad, I did not like it. My mom and I resisted. But he went ahead and prayed. I looked up at my mom, and she had a weird look on her face. My dad saw our reaction and got angry with us. And here is the sad thing: he never tried that again while we were living at home.

We tell this story as a warning. Make sure that you prepare the ground for new spiritual habits and practices. Husbands and wives are best advised to agree on new habits together. Not only is it good to seek prior agreement; parents should also develop a mindset that you will establish the family habit and stick with it, even in the face of various forms of opposition that can arise from members of your family. Remember, opposition may be a form of spiritual attack. My dad experienced spiritual attack in trying to do a good thing, because he wasn't prepared. If he had been ready with a good plan and the right mindset, he could have started a great family habit.

I (Chad) see the beautiful redemption in this story, though, from the perspective of a son and a grandson. Although my dad never learned how to pray from his father, God taught him how to do it anyway. He consistently led us as a family in prayer, but I have a special memory of seeing *my grandfather on his knees in prayer when I was in high school*. The doors to his bedroom were shut, with no one around, and I accidentally walked in on him while he was praying. He was alone, a man in his seventies, at peace with God in prayer. He developed a habit and now lives in it regularly. Now whenever we get together as an extended family, it is very important to him to lead a prayer for the family. Every holiday or family occasion, he initiates saying a prayer for the family gathering.

God never gave up on him as a spiritual parent, even though he had missed a great opportunity to lead his family in worship when his children were young. So no matter how old your kids are, it's never too late to start.

## GETTING STARTED
### Seeds Family Worship Devotion

Whether family worship is a new practice in your home or something you have been doing for years, we pray that this devotion might be a tool to help your family worship together at home.

We have divided each family worship experience into four sections that we believe are key components of effective family worship. Before you get started, we ask you to take a moment and read through the overview of each of these sections.

- *Prayer.* Pray the printed prayer together or create your own prayer as you begin your time together.
- *Praise.* This is an opportunity for your family to sing praises together. Mix it up and be creative during this time. Your involvement is key to your child's engagement.

- *Word.* This is a focused time during which your family gets to hear and respond to God's Word. Don't feel like you have to answer every question.
- *Walk.* This section outlines ideas to help your family walk out your faith and apply the principles you have learned together from the Bible.

Our prayer is that family worship will be your child's favorite time!

## MORE THAN CONQUERORS
### Prayer
*Pray this prayer out loud:* "Jesus, thank you for dying for our sins and conquering death through your resurrection. Thank you for loving us just the way we are. Prepare our hearts to hear your Word. In your name we pray, amen."

### Praise
*Listen and respond:* Gather the family together and listen to "More Than Conquerors" (Rom. 8:37), from the album *Seeds of Character* (Seeds Family Worship). Be creative with what you do while you listen to the song. For example, maybe have a dance party or eat a favorite dessert together while you listen. Make sure to sing along, once you know the melody.

### Word
*Read:* In the book of Romans, chapter 8, Paul is writing to the church in Rome. The leaders of this church were struggling to understand the freedom we receive when we choose to follow Jesus. They believed that people

still had to follow the Old Testament laws in order for God to love them and in order to have relationship with him.

*Read Romans 8:28, 35, 37–39 out loud:* "We know that for those who love God all things work together for good, for those who are called according to his purpose.... Who shall separate us from the love of Christ? Shall tribulation, or distress, or persecution, or famine, or nakedness, or danger, or sword?... No, in all these things we are more than conquerors through him who loved us. For I am sure that neither death nor life, nor angels nor rulers, nor things present nor things to come, nor powers, nor height nor depth, nor anything else in all creation, will be able to separate us from the love of God in Christ Jesus our Lord" (ESV).

Paul wanted the church in Rome to know that, no matter what they faced in life, nothing could separate them from God's love in Christ Jesus. Because Jesus conquered sin on the cross and rose from the dead, nothing they could go through would keep them from the gift of salvation and God's unconditional love.

*Discuss these questions together:*

1. What do you think Paul means when he says we are "more than conquerors"?
   - *To conquer means to win or to defeat. In the context of Romans 8 as a whole, Paul is saying that sin, death, and suffering have no power over us because of what Jesus has done.*

84

2. How does it make you feel to know that there is nothing that can separate you from the love of God?
   • *Various answers.*

3. What attitudes or actions come from knowing that Christ loves us and wants a relationship with us enough to pay the penalty for our sins?
   • *Gratitude; obedience; love others the way Christ loves us.*

4. What are some ways we, as a family, can show Christ's unconditional love to people around us?
   • *Model Christ's love through the way we treat each other; watch a young family's kids so the parents can have a date night; serve in a ministry at our church; and so on.*

5. What is one thing you are wondering about because of what we have been learning?
   • *Various answers.*

*Ideas for walking out this Scripture passage:*

   • Practice creating an environment of unconditional love in your home by offering grace and forgiving one another.
   • Take turns praying this blessing over one another this week: "In all things, you are more than a conqueror through Christ Jesus, who loves you, and there is nothing that can separate you from the love of God in Christ Jesus our Lord. Amen."

*This week as a family, we are going to put Romans 8:37 into action by:*

- *Various answers.*

## Walk

*Engage in the following activity together. Supplies needed: strips of colorful paper, markers, tape or stapler.*

1. Have each person take three strips of paper and write on them things they struggle with or trials they are going through (things they sometimes are afraid might separate them from God's love).
2. Staple or tape each person's links together to make a single chain. One by one, read aloud what is written on each person's strip of paper. Explain that because of Jesus, there is nothing that can keep us from God's love.
3. Allow each person to break their chain as you read Romans 8:37–39. For a bigger challenge, have each person say Romans 8:37 from memory before they break their chain.

# DEDICATION IN ACTION

REMEMBER. It's a challenge to start a new habit like family worship, but this is important for cultivating other spiritual habits with your family.

CONSIDER. What do you need to begin family worship? We have several resources to consider.

- *The Beginner's Bible* (*www.beginnersbible.com*)
- *The Jesus Storybook Bible* (*www.jesusstorybookbible.com*)
- What's in the Bible? (DVD series) (*www.whatsinthebible.com*)
- *Seeds Family Worship* resources (*www.seedsfamilyworship.com*)

Take time to find your family worship fingerprint. You can learn as you go, so don't worry about getting it perfect at first. Start off with a good plan or a good resource so you can hit the ground running.

PRAY. Ask the Lord how your family can begin family worship in a way that works for you and for your family's unique design.

RESPOND. How is the Holy Spirit leading you *today* to live out your dedication to God in family worship?

LISTEN. "More Than Conquerors" (Rom. 8:37), *Seeds of Character*, Seeds Family Worship.

# CHAPTER 6

# DEDICATED TO THE WORD

"THE SUM OF YOUR WORD IS TRUTH, and every one of your righteous rules endures forever" (Ps. 119:160 ESV). Most of us take it for granted that everyday measurements are accurate. We trust people who package products and sell them to us, having faith that they are reliably giving us what they advertise on the packaging. But have you ever wondered

- whether you really got ten gallons the last time you filled your car with gasoline?
- whether you really got a quart of milk at the grocery store?
- whether that package of cornflakes really had twenty ounces in it?

Few people realize that there is an organization responsible for regulating measurements. It's called the International Bureau of Weights and Measures, and they make sure that we have accurate standards for weighing and measuring. They have a team of scientists who verify standards down to the weight of electrons. The organization was created in 1875 to ensure objective standards for the countries of the world.[1] It gives countries uniform weights and measures so that everyone can align with a single, objective standard.

The same is true in the world of music. Musicians have an objective standard when they tune an instrument. A guitarist tunes his guitar to 440 Hz in order to play an A note. To be in tune, you must comply with this standard, which has been established so that everyone can play together.

In a similar way, the God who created us has established objective standards that tell us what is good, what is right, and what is wrong. We trust that our Creator knows what is best, how our lives can make beautiful music when played correctly. He sets the standard, and we must tune ourselves to his Word. As parents, we want this for our children as well. We want what is best for them, but our understanding of *best* is often skewed by the different standards of our culture. People tend to value different things and have different understandings of right and wrong, good and evil, based on their cultural background, how they were raised, and their experiences. Fortunately, God doesn't leave this up to us. As disciples of Jesus, we can know the standards God has determined for our lives, because God has revealed them to us in his Word.

We recommend that parents follow the advice God gave to Joshua. God wanted Joshua not only to know the Word but also to meditate on it—all the time. In this way, Joshua would be careful to live it out. God told Joshua, "This Book of the Law shall not depart from your mouth, but you shall meditate on it day and night, so that you may be careful to do according to all that is written in it. For then you will make your way prosperous, and then you will have good success" (Josh. 1:8 ESV).

It is immensely important for parents to believe that parenting should be based on God's standard, his Word. If this is true, it means that we need to understand these standards and use them to define success for our children. That is why it is so essential for children to read God's Word, understand it, meditate on it, and apply it to their lives. Second Timothy 3:14–17 is an excellent place to begin for understanding the nature and purpose of Scripture: "As for you, continue in what you have learned and have become convinced of, because you know those from whom you learned it, and how from infancy you have known the Holy Scriptures, which are able to make you wise for salvation through faith in Christ Jesus. All Scripture is God-breathed and is useful for teaching, rebuking, correcting and training in righteousness, so that the servant of God may be thoroughly equipped for every good work."

In this passage are five key elements regarding the Scriptures. We want to unpack them in this chapter and show how they are useful for parents. These elements frame how we think about teaching Scripture. This passage also contains a progression showing how spiritual parenting works. In one sentence, this passage describes how Scripture came (1) through a parent, (2) to a child, (3) from God, (4) for salvation, and (5) for life. Let's break this down in detail.

1. *"You know those from whom you learned it"* (through a parent). Paul told Timothy, a young minister, to continue in what he had learned as a child. Notice how Paul reminds Timothy of the integrity of the people from whom he learned it, speaking of his mother and grandmother. These women had lived such exemplary lives that Paul could point to them as examples that would help Timothy continue to believe God's Word.

2. *"From infancy you have known the Holy Scriptures"* (to a child). Timothy was blessed to have been taught God's Word from the time he was an infant. He was grounded in the teaching and standards that God had given to his people. This is a wonderful reminder that if you teach your children the Word from the time they are young, it will give them a sense of purpose and guidance that will bless them their entire lives.

*3. "Scripture is God-breathed"* (from God). According to this passage, God inspired the Bible and "breathed into" it. That's another way of saying Scripture finds its origin in God, so we can know that Scripture is reliable (see also 2 Peter 1:20–21). God himself inspired the people who wrote the Bible, which means you can lean on it and trust it.

*4. "[Scripture is] to make you wise for salvation through faith in Christ Jesus"* (for salvation). There are many uses for Scripture, but we want to encourage you primarily to use Scripture as a tool that can make your children wise for salvation. Parents want to remember that of everything that is in the Bible, nothing is more important than Christ Jesus and the path of salvation.

*5. "[Scripture is] for teaching, rebuking, correcting and training in righteousness"* (for life). As we just mentioned, the primary purpose of Scripture is to understand God's gift of salvation through faith in Jesus. God gives his Word to us for direction and guidance, to help us grow and mature in our faith. God blesses us with the knowledge of his path and what is right and wrong. Old Testament scholar John Willis summed up the intention of God's instruction in the Torah, which is God's law: "The Old Testament word *torah* means instruction, guidance, or direction for an individual or community.... The spirit of the biblical idea is that God (out of his deep love for man) desires to give man guidance so that his life can be as full and complete as possible.... God's law (guidance) for man is a natural expression of his love, grace, mercy, and forgiveness."[2]

This means that we want to be careful to follow what God has established in the Bible. Scripture guides and blesses—when we feel like it, and when we don't; when it suits us, and when it doesn't; when we are ready for it, and when we are not.

Scripture is *useful* for parents. God gave us his written Word, and he expects people in authority (parents, in this case) to use Scripture for their children's well-being. The Bible informs our children's faith and equips them for everything God will call them to do. Without Scripture, we lose perspective and power.

It is difficult for a child to develop a love for reading the Bible if the parent does not share this love. Fortunately, God gave me (Bobby) a strong desire to know his Word early on. When I first believed and trusted Christ, I could not get enough of reading the Bible. I had a deep yearning to know God's truth and God's ways. If you, as a parent, can honestly say that you do not have this desire right now, the first thing I recommend for you is to ask God

CHAD: I have learned more about the Word from my mom and dad's teaching at home than from all my dad's sermons combined. That's not to say that he preaches bad sermons! It's simply saying that the true impact of his teaching was at home. As my sister and I look back, our parents impacted us most by who they were in the spontaneous, everyday situations. We could see that our parents loved God and his Word, because it was a part of their lives as a whole, not just on Sunday mornings.

Whenever my sister or I had a question, my dad always knew *exactly* where the Bible addressed the issue at hand. It was like magic. But he never just gave us the answer. He would say to us, "Go get your Bible." He'd let us read for ourselves what God had to say about our question. This taught me the discipline of going to the Bible for answers.

My sister remembers every Bible our parents gave her, even the picture Bibles from childhood. My parents created an environment in our home where God cultivated the seed of his Word in our lives, where the Word of God was a part of casual conversation. Of all the gifts my parents gave me, the one I'm most thankful for is that they helped foster in me a personal love for God's Word, by showing me that they loved the Word.

for it. It is difficult to lead your children in loving God's Word if that is not something you love as well. My kids were blessed to have a mother who walks with God. On a regular basis as they grew up in our home, they would see her reading her Bible, praying, and caring for others. Did we have faults as parents? We sure did! We had our share of control issues and arguments. But we are grateful to God that he let our children see that we were genuinely seeking to live our lives as people trying to trust and follow Jesus.

## THE WORD OF GOD IS LIVING

"The word of God is living and active," says the writer of Hebrews (4:12 ESV). In Christian cultures today, many people fixate on the *reliability and trustworthiness* of the written Word of God but forget the immense *power* of God's spoken word. God not only speaks to us through the written Word as we read it; he also speaks to us fresh every day as we remember it. His Word is not dead.

God's words are powerful to encourage us and help us obey. They pierce our hearts. That's why the writer of Hebrews says that the word of God is "sharper than any two-edged sword, piercing to the division of soul and of spirit, of joints and of marrow, and discerning the thoughts and intentions of the heart" (4:12 ESV). The Word is more than just words on a page; it's powerful and real. It's not just a book to be read; it's a voice to be heard.

This is encouraging to parents because it means that you have the power of God's Word with you wherever you go. You speak the Word, not just read it to your children. The Word is useful in your regular, everyday life. For example, when you are sitting on the couch watching a movie, and something questionable comes up, you can say, "What does God's Word say about that?" You can speak truth into your children's lives based on what you know from Scripture. This is biblical training in the Word.

# THE WORD IS BEAUTIFUL

The Bible dedicates an entire song—Psalm 119—to the awesomeness of God's Word. It's the longest chapter of the Bible. The poet describes digging deep into God's Word. These verses sing of the goodness of passionately seeking God in his Word. Read these excerpts from Psalm 119 (with a summary word above each passage) and let the Word of God speak for itself.

### PURITY

How can a young man keep his way pure?
    By guarding it according to your word.
With my whole heart I seek you;
    let me not wander from your commandments!
I have stored up your word in my heart,
    that I might not sin against you.

*—vv. 9–11 ESV*

### REVELATION

Open my eyes, that I may behold
    wondrous things out of your law.
I am a sojourner on the earth;
    hide not your commandments from me!

*—vv. 18–19 ESV*

### COUNSEL

Your testimonies are my delight;
    they are my counselors.

*—v. 24 ESV*

### HOPE

Let your steadfast love come to me, O Lord,
    your salvation according to your promise;
then shall I have an answer for him who taunts me,
    for I trust in your word.
And take not the word of truth utterly out of my mouth,
    for my hope is in your rules.

*—vv. 41–43 ESV*

## RICHES

It is good for me that I was afflicted,
    that I might learn your statutes.
The law of your mouth is better to me
    than thousands of gold and silver pieces.

*—vv. 71–72 ESV*

## DIRECTION

How sweet are your words to my taste,
    sweeter than honey to my mouth!
Through your precepts I get understanding;
    therefore I hate every false way.
Your word is a lamp to my feet
    and a light to my path.

*—vv. 103–5 ESV*

## KNOWLEDGE

Your testimonies are wonderful;
    therefore my soul keeps them.
The unfolding of your words gives light;
    it imparts understanding to the simple.

*—vv. 129–30 ESV*

## TRUTH

The sum of your word is truth,
    and every one of your righteous rules endures forever.

*—v. 160 ESV*

Each of these passages from Psalm 119 shows us the timeless beauty of God's Word. The Word empowers us to avoid sin as we store it in our hearts. It opens our eyes to see God's wonder. It is our great counselor, our hope, our purpose in affliction, a lamp to our feet as it illuminates our way. It is our spiritual food.

Why are we spiritually weak and weary and discouraged at times? Have we eaten the Word that gives life to our souls? Our families are desperate for God to speak. And he has spoken and continues to speak to us through his Word!

Why is the Word of God so important? As disciples of Jesus,

we are dedicated to the Word because Jesus was dedicated to the Word. He lived out the truth that all Scripture comes from God and is useful for every good work (2 Tim. 3:16–17). As families, we follow after him by listening to God's voice as he did.

## JESUS AND THE WORD

From a young age, Jesus immersed himself in Scripture, even spending four days as a twelve-year-old boy apart from his parents in the house of God, dialoguing with teachers of the Bible (Luke 2:41–48). His parents found him in the temple listening and asking questions about God's Word.

Looking at his life later, as he began his ministry, we learn that Jesus had hidden God's Word in his heart. During his temptation in the desert, he quoted Scripture from memory: "It is written, 'Man shall not live by bread alone, but by every word that comes from the mouth of God'" (Matt. 4:4 ESV). This quotation comes from Deuteronomy 8:3, a passage Jesus heard in synagogue growing up. The people of God did not have personal Bibles at their disposal until long after Guttenberg's printing press; they had to memorize the Word!

Jesus was dedicated to and formed by God's Word, and one of the tasks of a dedicated parent is to raise children to be men and women of the Word. Then, when they are tempted with power, prestige, and shortcutting in their obedience to God, they will have the power of God's Word stored in their hearts. Our goal as spiritual parents is that our children love the Word of God for themselves.

## DEDICATION TO THE WORD IN OUR HOMES

Almost every in-depth analysis of the state of discipleship in the church today points to the supreme need for people to get into the Word of God and apply it to their lives.[3] Recently, the Willow Creek Association, one of the most influential church groups in

America, published the results of some very interesting studies about spiritual growth and development. They surveyed more than 250,000 people in more than 1,000 churches. The chairman of the association, Bill Hybels, notes, "We learned that the most effective strategy for moving people forward in their journey of faith is biblical engagement. Not just getting people into the Bible when they're in church—which we do quite well—but helping them engage the Bible on their own outside of church."[4]

From what we've seen over years of pastoring, there is a strong correlation between a child's faith and their parents' devotion to the Word. It's amazing the difference a parent's example makes in a child's life. The battle starts with you as a parent—God is calling you, right now, to get into the Word. Even if you are active in attending church and occasionally read the Bible, it's vital that you are an engaged reader, a student of the Word. Sometimes people settle for what they think the Bible says, but it's vital for every parent—for every *family*—to know what the Bible actually says. Here are three practical ways to get started.

- Share the Word with your children.
- Pray with your children to understand the Word.
- Memorize the Word with your children.

## 1. Share the Word

The apostle Paul points out that it is impossible to believe in Jesus Christ until we hear the message about Jesus. To believe the gospel and trust Jesus, people need exposure to the Word. Paul writes, "How then will they call on him in whom they have not believed? And how are they to believe in him of whom they have never heard? And how are they to hear without someone preaching? ... So faith comes from hearing, and hearing through the word of Christ" (Rom. 10:14, 17 ESV).

Like the people who needed to hear the message in Paul's day, our children need to hear the message about Christ today. After all, "faith comes from hearing." We give our children opportunities to hear the Word of God by teaching them how to read the Bible for themselves. We do it by listening with them to teachings from a pastor or children's minister and allowing the Holy Spirit to transform their hearts. There are many, many ways to hear the Word with your children, but the important thing is that they are exposed to the Word in a way they can understand. Exposure to the teachings of Jesus is an essential factor in faith development and spiritual growth for children.

Sadly, we often meet parents who have come to us because their teenage children are struggling with their faith. More often than not, the root issue is a lack of exposure to the Word of God. Again, we're not just talking about going to a youth group or attending Sunday services. Children need regular exposure to the Word in the home, reading and discussing the Bible with their parents. Faith is not something that automatically develops when a child is born to Christian parents. It is the Word that creates faith. Listen to how famous nineteenth-century Christian leader D. L. Moody describes it happening in his life: "I prayed for Faith, and thought that some day Faith would come down and strike me like lightning. But Faith did not seem to come. One day I read in the tenth chapter of Romans.... I had closed my Bible, and prayed for Faith. I now opened my Bible, and began to study, and Faith has been growing ever since."[5]

We have observed that people who spend regular time in God's Word tend to develop faith, just as Moody did. So one of the most important things parents can do to help children develop faith is to get them into the habit of reading God's Word. Our desire as spiritual parents is that our children learn to love the Word of God for themselves. And so we share the Word with them in the hope that they will take hold of it.

I (Chad) remember when my own spiritual transformation began. Until this point, my parents had read the Bible with my sister and me, but then I began to enjoy reading the Word on my own. This is the goal for parents with their children when it comes to reading God's Word. It happened for me as I was reading his Word in the eighth grade. I had just started reading the Bible on my own, waking up thirty minutes early each day to read and journal through the Gospels. I continued on, reading through the rest of the New Testament. This experience of daily reading each morning helped me to truly see Jesus in a way I never had before, and my faith started to grow, becoming something I owned for myself for the first time in my life. My parents' love for the Word truly became my love for the Word. I identified with the stories I read by putting myself on the sea as Peter walked across the waters of the Sea of Galilee; on the path when the centurion asked Jesus to heal his servant; in the crowd during the feeding of the five thousand. Reading the Bible opened the eyes of my heart to the person of Jesus, so I could see him for who he really is, and this sustained me when things got tough later in high school.

## 2. Pray to Understand the Word

The Holy Spirit enables us to be receptive to the Word, so we should pray for the Spirit's guidance. The Spirit brings to life the teaching of the Bible and enables us to develop a spiritual mind. The apostle Paul puts it this way: "The person without the Spirit does not accept the things that come from the Spirit of God but considers them foolishness, and cannot understand them because they are discerned only through the Spirit" (1 Cor. 2:14).

The truths of the Christian faith seem like foolishness to non-Christians. And our children can be like non-Christians in this way as well. Simply hearing the Word is not enough to change a heart and lead to lasting transformation. In addition to sharing the Word with our children, we must pray for the Spirit's presence and guidance to help them *understand* God's Word.

On the other hand, we sometimes meet teenagers and new

Christians who simply and easily grasp profound biblical teachings. They not only grasp them; they clearly see how to apply these teachings to their lives. The difference, again, is the indwelling presence of God's Spirit. With the Holy Spirit inside you, the Bible comes to life! The famous reformer Martin Luther described his experience this way: "The Bible is alive, it speaks to me. It has feet, it runs after me. It has hands, it lays hold of me."[6]

## 3. Memorize the Word

Throughout the history of the church, one of the most common practices of dedicated parents has been to engage their children with the memorization of Scripture. Consider this amazing truth: having your own *personal* Bible is a new reality for Christians. For most of church history (and even in most parts of the world today), people did not have the Word in their homes, accessible at any time. Since access to the Word was limited, they had to find creative ways to memorize it. Think of the opportunities we have today to store Scripture in our hearts!

Many passages of the Bible recommend the practice of memorization. This habit not only enables our children to know God's direction but also helps embed God's truth into the way they think. Here is one passage among many, from the first chapter of the book of Psalms: "His delight is in the law of the Lord, and on his law he meditates day and night" (Ps. 1:2 ESV).

The ministry that I (Jason) belong to has tried to make Scripture memorization as simple and easy as possible for parents. We have found that combining short portions of the Word of God with catchy songs is incredibly helpful. There is something about music that helps us to remember words. Think of all those silly commercial jingles you still remember from watching television as a child. They stick with you, even when you wish you could forget them.

The same is true (in a positive and life-changing way) when you combine Scripture with song and teach children to memorize it. Over and over again, I am encouraged by parents who have listened to the Seeds Family Worship music that we produce. They share with us how they are filled with joy because their kids are learning God's Word. They look in the rearview mirror in their car as they drive and see their kids *singing* Scripture. Their joy comes from knowing that their children are storing God's Word in their hearts (Ps. 119:11). Many parents have been brought to tears by hearing their children singing the Word. Music is one of the easiest and most powerful ways to memorize Scripture.

And there is an added benefit from teaching your children to memorize Scripture in this way. Countless parents have told me that they are amazed at how many Scriptures *they* now know by heart, all from listening to our songs with their kids. From the very beginning of Seeds Family Worship, our desire has been that families would not just sing the songs but also memorize the Word to give them strength and fill them with power for life. We have free resources on our website to help families accomplish this. You can print Scripture memory cards for all of the Seeds Family Worship songs. Anyone can stream the songs and print out the verses from our website for free. Then you can post the verses around your house and challenge each other to memorize them together.

There are other ways to memorize Scripture as well. In addition to learning Scripture through song, you can teach your children to memorize the Bible using technology or note cards. There are some great smart phone applications, like *Fighter Verses* and *Memory Verse*. These are just two apps that can help parents and children memorize God's Word together.

You can get creative and find a method that works for you, but remember, there are no shortcuts to this process; it will take effort and time. But that investment has a wonderful return. One of the blessings of memorizing Scripture is that you can come back to the Word later in life, often when you least expect it. Learning the Word is part of being formed into the image of Christ. Psalm 1 says that people who meditate on God's Word are "like a tree planted by streams of water, which yields its fruit in season and whose leaf does not wither" (Ps. 1:3). Memorizing the Word and meditating on it is a life-giving process that, God promises us, will eventually bear fruit—for days, months, and years to come. It may even have an impact on your family's subsequent generations. Small investments of time and energy today can change the future.

## CONCLUSION

Many years ago, I (Bobby) developed a serious relationship with a young lady I had recently met named Cindy. Cindy lived in Memphis, Tennessee, and for that summer I was working for my father's company in Calgary, Canada. We had a long-distance relationship. At that time, making long-distance phone calls was very expensive. Email hadn't yet been invented, so to stay in touch and keep up the relationship, we often wrote each other letters—yes, handwritten letters. I remember how each day I would look forward to the arrival of the mail, hoping there would be a letter from Cindy.

Whenever a letter from her arrived, I would read through it several times, enjoying every sentence, wondering what meanings were hidden behind her words. I still have all of these letters today, even though this was more than thirty-five years ago.

Why did I spend so much time reading these simple letters from Cindy? Since we couldn't be together that summer, these letters were the means by which I got to know this young woman. Through her letters, I learned who she was. In the letters, it felt like she was present with me, even though we were separated by more than two thousand miles. Through the letters we wrote, our relationship deepened and developed so much so that, by the time we met up again after the three months of summer vacation, I was ready to ask her to be my wife.

The Bible is like this. It's like a letter written by God to us (although it is much more than a letter, of course). Because I wanted to know Cindy, it was exciting to get a letter from her. In the same way, God's Word is exciting. We soak up every word that comes from our Father, because we want to know him. By reading the Bible, we learn more and more about God, and he truly does become present with us as we study his words through the gift of the Holy Spirit. As we seek God through Scripture, we not only know him better; we develop a relationship with him. Then, the more and more we study it, we will come to know, experience, and love him in deeper and deeper ways.

## DEDICATION IN ACTION

REMEMBER. Memorize 2 Timothy 3:16–17 as a family.

All Scripture is God-breathed and is useful for teaching, rebuking, correcting and training in righteousness, so that the servant of God may be thoroughly equipped for every good work.

CONSIDER. How can you share, pray, and memorize God's Word as a family?

PRAY. Ask God to give you discipline and understanding as you seek him through his Word.

RESPOND. How is the Holy Spirit leading you *today* to live out your dedication to God in the Word?

LISTEN. "Delight" (Ps. 1), *Seeds of Character*, Seeds Family Worship.

# CHAPTER 7

# DEDICATED TO PRAYER

**JESUS LIVED A PRAYERFUL LIFE.** He woke up early in the morning to pray, he prayed before he ate, he prayed before making important decisions, he prayed for his disciples, and he prayed for little children. In fact, everything Jesus said came from the Father, and everything he did was pleasing to the Father (John 8:28–29). Jesus enjoyed perfect union with God, and the good news is that we are called into a similar relationship with the Father through Jesus, having been adopted into God's family. We have an intimate connection to the Father, and in this relationship with him, we can learn to be good earthly fathers and mothers.

For many people, prayer is something that takes two or three minutes before a meal or before bedtime. But prayer is far more than giving God a nod five minutes out of the day; it's a lifestyle of communication with God. Living prayerfully is something that we integrate into our lives. We are constantly aware of our need for God, asking him for his guidance, seeking his help, and thanking him when we have reason to celebrate his love and his goodness. When we run into difficulties, we pray; when we experience great joys, we pray; and when we face uncertainty, we pray. Our lives are a continual prayer to God.

## JESUS' PRAYER

Parents need to pray for their children. That's a nonnegotiable. If you aren't praying for your children, start today! Many parents want to pray for their kids but aren't sure how to do it, how to get started. We want to suggest that Jesus gives us a model for this when he prays for his disciples in John 17. This passage highlights several principles that we can apply to praying for our children.

John 17 records the prayer conversation that Jesus has with his Father on the night before his crucifixion. Jesus knows that he is about to be taken away, beaten, and killed, leaving his disciples on their own, but before he goes, he cries out to God on their behalf. He pours out his soul in passionate prayer for them.

> I have manifested your name to the people whom you gave me out of the world. Yours they were, and you gave them to me, and they have kept your word. Now they know that everything that you have given me is from you.... Holy Father, keep them in your name, which you have given me, that they may be one, even as we are one. While I was with them, I kept them in your name, which you have given me. I have guarded them, and not one of them has been lost except the son of destruction, that the Scripture might be fulfilled. But now I am coming to you, and these things I speak in the world, that they may have my joy fulfilled in themselves. I have given them your word, and the world has hated them because they are not of the world, just as I am not of the world. I do not ask that you take them out of the world, but that you keep them from the evil one. They are not of the world, just as I am not of the world. Sanctify them in the truth; your word is truth. As you sent me into the world, so I have sent them into the world. And for their sake I consecrate myself, that they also may be sanctified in truth.
>
> —John 17:6–7, 11–19 ESV

There is a lot packed into these verses. But how do we apply these words of Jesus to our prayers for our kids? Let's take a closer look, going through Jesus' prayer verse by verse.

1. *"You gave them to me" (v. 6).* First, we should note that Jesus acknowledges that his disciples (read this word as "children," to help apply this principle to your family) were a gift from God. We suggest that you begin your prayers for your children by remembering that God created them, gave them to you as a gift, and loves them even more than you do. Starting this way changes the way you think about your children, so that you see them not as a burden or an annoyance but as a precious gift to be treasured. When we remember that children are a gift from God, we don't take them for granted. We see parenting them as an honor and a privilege, not another task on our "to do" list.

2. *"I do not ask that you take them out of the world" (v. 15).* Second, though Jesus loves his disciples and doesn't want them to be harmed by his enemies, he does not pray for God to take his disciples out of the world. Some parents tend to be overprotective of their children, and for good reasons. The world is not a safe or friendly place for kids. And parents need to guard their children and protect them from evil. But we also need to remember that though this world will pose challenges for your children, they are not called out of the world; they are called into the dark places of the world. If your children grow to become followers of Jesus, the world will hate them just like it hated the disciples. That's a promise Jesus makes to his disciples—the battle will come to them eventually (John 15:20). Given the battle for your children's souls, it's vital to pray for their physical, emotional,

and spiritual safety. And we trust God's purposes even when they get hurt. But we cannot hide them from the world. Pray that God will give you wisdom to guide your children as they interact with the world, develop friendships, and grow to discover God's unique call on their lives.

3. *"Keep them from the evil one" (v. 15).* Third, Jesus prays for protection, specifically against Satan. Jesus asks for this because he is leaving his disciples and will no longer be physically present with them: "While I was with them, I protected them" (v. 12 NIV). Similarly, we must pray for our children's protection, both physically and spiritually, for the times when we cannot be present with them. If our children align their lives with Christ, the world will misunderstand and persecute them. The enemy will use anything and everything to destroy them (1 Peter 5:8). As we mentioned in the previous paragraph, we cannot (and should not) remove our children from interaction with the world, but we can pray for God to shield them and protect them from the evil one.

4. *"Sanctify them in the truth; your word is truth" (v. 17).* Finally, Jesus prays for sanctification. The word *sanctify* isn't a common word today. It means "to be set apart" or designated as holy. In the Old Testament, things and people were sanctified, or set apart, for God and his purposes. The implements employed in temple worship were set apart for special use. Priests were set apart, dedicated to lead the people in worship. And the entire nation of Israel was set apart, made holy, dedicated to God's purposes in redeeming the world through the coming Savior and King, Jesus. Another word for *sanctify* brings us to the title of this book.

> Sanctifying something or someone means consecrating or "dedicating" them to God and his purposes. This is what Hannah and Elkanah did with their son Samuel — they dedicated him to the Lord.

In his prayer in John 17, Jesus is asking his Father to set his disciples apart, to "dedicate" them.[1] When someone is sanctified, they are included in the inner circle of holiness. In this case, that inner circle is the relationship between God the Father and God the Son. Jesus, the Son of God, prays for us to be dedicated to God and included in this intimate relationship on two levels.

1. He asks God to dedicate his disciples (v. 17).
2. Jesus dedicates himself to the disciples (v. 19).

Jesus prays that God will sanctify the disciples, giving them a purpose that aligns with Jesus' own mission on earth. And Jesus dedicates himself to his disciples, praying and declaring that he will commit himself to them, to meeting their needs and being with them. Our relationship with God is directly connected to these two dedications made by God the Father and God the Son. Jesus committed himself to dying on the cross, sacrificing himself for our sakes so that we could be freed to bring the gospel to the world. The only way we can come into the inner circle is through Jesus.

Throughout the gospel of John, Jesus has maintained a close relationship with his Father, and now he is asking God to share that closeness with his disciples. This is what Jesus' prayer of dedication means. He is asking God to bring the disciples into the inner circle of their relationship. While parental relationships can never replace a child's relationship with God, we can learn to model our parenting after the way God relates with us. Take some time to do what Jesus did here in John 17: ask God to set your kids apart as holy to God. Let God know that you are making this commitment. And like Jesus, pray that God will keep them and make them into all he meant them to be. This is a prayer that God will not ignore. It reflects the very heart of Jesus and the will of the Father.

Jesus' prayer offers us a beautiful model of how we can seek God for the sake of our children. Spend time reading and meditating on the words of Jesus, and allow God's Word, through these verses, to shape your prayers for your kids. Let's empower and protect our children with prayer and release them into the world, just like Jesus did with his disciples!

# LEARNING TO PRAY

It is one thing to look at how Jesus prayed, but it is another thing to pray like he prayed. Most of us are just beginners in this, still learning the art of praying. And it's okay to start simple. In fact, simple prayers are often the best when they are honest and come from the heart. People who pray simple, earnest, and regular prayers are people whom God uses to change the world.

Early in my own parenting journey with my wife, Cindy, I (Bobby) learned the importance of prayer from a family in our church, the Ruckers. When Cindy and I were expecting our first child, we began looking around at the parents in our church and studying them to see what they did. We looked for parents who had raised godly kids, especially those who were part of extended families with several generations of godly people. Almost every congregation has people like this, if you take the time to look for them. Since I was the lead pastor of the church, we had a great vantage point, and it was interesting to learn about these families and hear their stories. We asked them what they did to disciple and train their kids in the Lord, and what they considered to be the most critical factor in the faith development of their extended family.

All of them said the same thing. Prayer.

John and Ruth Rucker were legends at a nearby church in the

Nashville area. They had been faithful Christians serving and leading in that church for several decades. John had served for a long
time as an elder in a church that he and Ruth had helped plant
in the Nashville area, and for thirty-five years they had led the
well-respected Otter Creek Kindergarten. The kindergarten had a
reputation throughout Nashville for making a profound spiritual
impact on young children. Country stars, Christian musicians,
and just plain old regular folks like us all wanted to enroll our kids
at Ruth's school. Because of Ruth's leadership at the school, there
was a palpable spiritual presence intertwined throughout the educational program. Ruth knew kids and she understood parents.

Most important, John and Ruth had raised six children in the
Lord, plus three foster children. They had thirty grandchildren.
And by the grace of God, all of their children and grandchildren
had become faithful Christians and were serving and leading in
local churches.

When I interviewed the Ruckers, they were in their eighties.
As I was preparing for the interview, I expected to take pages of
notes detailing all of their advice and wisdom, but the secret to
their success was far less complicated than I imagined. Ruth said it
several times during our conversation, that everything came down
to one thing: prayer. "We prayed every day for our kids," she said.
"We prayed every day for our grandkids. We prayed every day for
the children in the kindergarten. And we asked other people to
join us in prayer. It wasn't me. God answered our prayers. If we
could point to the most important thing, it would be prayer."

Stories like this shouldn't surprise us. God promises us that he
will respond to our prayers, and we know that prayer is the primary means God has established to meet our needs and answer our
requests. Yet many parents do not pray for their children. Remember that prayer is not an obligation, a duty we must fulfill to earn
God's favor. God wants to hear from his children simply because
he loves us. So when you come to him about *your* children, know

that he's already interested in what you have to say. You don't need to speak in a formal tone or explain every detail. You can simply ask the Father for help, wisdom, and guidance. Talk to him about the things you worry about with your kids. Let him know where you are struggling as a parent, where you need help. "Ask, and it will be given to you," Jesus said. "Seek, and you will find; knock, and it will be opened to you" (Matt. 7:7 ESV). As you learn to pray, it's important to recognize the different methods of and contexts for prayer. A great way to start your journey toward God in prayer is to learn how to pray alone.

## Pray Alone

Prayer is a simple conversation with God. You don't need special training to pray. Start right where you are today. Jesus told us, "When you pray, go into your room and shut the door and pray to your Father who is in secret. And your Father who sees in secret will reward you" (Matt. 6:6 ESV). Though there are many ways you can pray, a simple place to start is to just go into your room alone and begin talking to God like you would talk to a close friend.

Even Jesus needed regular time with the Father before he could minister to others. If you become distracted while you are alone, read some Scripture first to focus your mind on God and his promises. The book of Psalms, with 150 written prayers, is a great place to start. These times of prayer while you are alone will be a constant source of strength for you as a parent.

## Pray with Your Spouse

Many couples—even those with healthy relationships—find it challenging to pray together. So don't get discouraged if you find this difficult. But just because it's hard doesn't mean you shouldn't do it. Even the smallest efforts you put into praying with your spouse can yield huge benefits, for both your marriage and your kids. Each time before he leaves, Jason puts his arm around his wife and prays a short (twenty seconds!) prayer of protection and blessing for her. When Bobby and Cindy turn off the lights and say goodnight, they reach for each other's hands and say a short prayer, including a prayer for their kids. Find what works for you and then make it a habit.

Again, this doesn't have to be complicated. Prayer is simply talking to God, and with practice, you and your spouse will begin to feel comfortable doing this together. If you're a single parent (or you *feel* like a single parent), find a prayer partner to pray with you. Ask someone in your church or small group to meet with you once a week to pray for your children.

## Pray with Your Kids

Praying with your children can also be quite challenging. The first time you try, one child will start crying, another will laugh, and you may find yourself yelling instead of praying. Don't give up!

There are several easy ways to build family prayers into your daily schedule, but one simple and practical method that works for almost anyone is to pray sentence prayers. Mark Holman suggests this in his book *Faith Begins at Home*. It's a straightforward pattern in which everyone takes a turn finishing a sentence in prayer.[2]

- "Lord, I thank you for ..."
- "Lord, forgive me for ..."
- "Lord, one of the fears I need help with is ..."

Try creating your own sentence prayers, and you'll be amazed at the immediate connection you'll feel as a family.

If you have small children, keep the prayers simple. Begin building prayer habits into your family culture when your kids are young. As they get older, they will have a history and habit of prayer, and it will be much easier for your family to pray together.

# Pray Around Your Kids

Your children watch *everything* you do.

When my (Bobby) son, Chad, was a little boy, he liked to play outside while I cut the grass. One day, as I wrapped up mowing, I saw Chad on the other side of the yard, keeping pace with his own toy lawn mower. We "mowed" together for several minutes.

When I finished, I began pushing the mower along the sidewalk to the front of the house. As I rounded the corner, I noticed a piece of grass in my mouth and turned to spit it out. At that moment, I saw Chad walking behind me. And at that same spot on the sidewalk, he turned his head and spat onto the pavement, just like his dad.

I never forgot that moment. If little eyes are watching us when we mow the lawn, copying what we do, how much more does this matter when we are doing things that matter for eternity?

Children learn by watching our example; we *must* be who we want them to be. And as my son, Chad, will say today, this translates into spiritual parenting, not just mowing the lawn.

Hearing my (Chad) parents pray for people had a huge impact on me. I saw that they had a real faith. My dad, as a pastor, often talked on the phone with people from the church, and I occasionally overheard his conversations. Often as they reached the end of the conversation — whether in the car or at home — he asked them, "Can I pray for you right now?" Then he prayed for them over the phone. My ears were listening.

As a child, I didn't think twice about it, because my dad did it all the time. Now I realize it's not all that normal, but I picked up the habit and continue doing it on occasion to this day, just like my father. My dad never sat me down and said, "Chad, when you're talking with someone on the phone, you should ask to pray with them," but I find myself doing what he did. I'm thankful that I was blessed to have a father who not only prayed for me but also taught me how to pray by example, not just in church on

Sunday mornings or at home before meals but also in the every-day situations of life, like talking on the phone with friends.

## Pray with Friends and Family

From the time our (Bobby) children were born, my wife and I prayed for them at least once a day until they turned eighteen. That's more than thirteen thousand prayers! But those weren't the only prayers prayed for them. We also asked friends and grand-parents to pray for our kids, and we dedicated each child during a service in our local church, where Christ's family agreed to pray for them as well. I like to joke that my kids never had a chance to escape the Lord; from the first day of their lives, they were covered in prayer.

Even if you have never prayed for your children, it's not too late to start. You can do this! God never intended for you to go it alone. And one of the reasons why he gave us the church is to encourage us and provide support from others. The Bible teaches us to ask our church family for help when we need godly advice and prayer.

Christian parents can build prayer support for their children through partnership with another family. Look for a family in your church with kids who are roughly the same age as yours, and covenant to pray daily for each other's children. I (Bobby) took this even one step farther and partnered with one of my close friends, David Sanders, not only to pray for each other's sons but also serve as another father figure to each other's boys. Single par-ents will need this help, and you need to have the courage to ask for it. Even if you do not have a spouse or if your spouse is not involved in your child's life, you can have other people join you in prayer.

You can also ask your church elders for prayer. James 5:14 encourages us to seek the help of people who have been chosen to serve as spiritual shepherds for our congregation. Our elders should be busy praying for the children in the church and witnessing God's miracles in their lives regularly.

## Pray during Crises and Special Occasions

Throughout our lives, there are times of crisis and need. When you and your family turn to God and pray during these times, God will stretch your faith. Praying together strengthens the family, bringing comfort and assurance during times of fear and uncertainty. Children learn how to relate to God and call on him during these experiences.

This past year, my family (Jason) had a ski trip planned with my brother's family the week after Christmas. We were fired up! We planned to drive from our home in Twin Falls, Idaho, to their new home in Midway, Utah. The trip usually takes about four hours, depending on the weather. Well, the weather slowed us down — to a crawl. It was snowing lightly when we left the house, but as soon as we got on the interstate, it grew intense. I told my wife we were in for a long trip. At that moment, *I remembered we had forgotten to pray when we left the house*, as we usually do before setting out on a trip like this. I sensed the Holy Spirit prompting me to pray. I turned off the radio and invited the family to ask the Lord for his protection as we made our way down the snow-covered roads.

Less than ten minutes later, a dense fog set in across the valley. As we crested a hill, we saw a long line of semis stopped in the road. They were at a complete standstill. I slammed on the brakes and prayed out loud for the Lord to help us stop before we hit the back of the eighteen-wheeler ahead of us. It was a miracle that we stopped in time, but that was just the beginning. I realized that we were now a target for the next vehicle to come over the hill. We began to hear crushing sounds of steel thundering behind us. We later learned a two-ton tow truck had smashed into an eighteen-wheeler. Cars and trucks began sliding off both sides of the interstate and colliding with each other.

I knew we had to move quickly. At this point, I was yelling my prayers to the Lord, crying out for him to protect us. I pulled to the left of a semi into a gap, but as I moved forward, another out-of-control eighteen-wheeler sped past us. The trailer hit the sliding back door of our van, behind me on the driver's side, where my eight-year-old daughter was sitting.

My daughter screamed, "Mommy, are we gonna die?" I felt the weight of the truck push us aside, but I didn't hear her words or even see the color of the truck as it rolled off the interstate into the barrow pit with several other crashed cars and eighteen-wheelers. I could think of only one thing—getting us through this to safety.

By God's grace, we were able to get over to the side of the road and out of harm's way. There was a twenty-car pileup all around us, with debris scattered over the interstate. When we stepped out of the van, the road was so slick that we almost fell to the ground. We thanked God for his mercy. We were all unhurt. It truly was a miracle.

CHAD: Every Thanksgiving, our family has a very meaningful tradition. Everyone finishes their meal, and then we all share one thing we are thankful for. We've done this as long as I can remember, and most of the time it ends up being somewhat emotional. We go around the table and tell everyone how God has blessed our life, or share a meaningful grace he's given us or a general thanks to God. Every year we say similar things—thanks for family, friends, a good job—but it's good just to have a time and place to tell the whole family what's on our heart. I look forward to hearing these prayers of thanks every year. They keep life in perspective and keep us rooted in gratitude to God—together.

We believed the Lord answered our prayers that winter morning. We also believed he wanted us to turn around and head back home, which we did. It was amazing that we were able to drive away from an accident like that.

I'll be the first to admit that I don't understand the mystery of prayer, how God works when he does, but I will say that I have seen God work over and over again through the years as we have called out to him when we've had needs.

In addition to praying during times of crisis, many families make a habit of praying on special occasions or holidays. In either case, whether you are establishing traditions of prayer at times of celebration or learning to call on God in crisis situations, you take advantage of God-given opportunities to highlight his presence in your midst. Seize the day and create the context for a meaningful prayer time. And while these moments are important, don't neglect what we talked about earlier—making prayer a part of your regular, daily life.

## THE DISCIPLES' PRAYER

In addition to the prayer we looked at earlier in this chapter, from John 17, there is another prayer that Jesus prays to teach his disciples how to pray. Quite often, people refer to this prayer in Matthew 6 as the Lord's Prayer. And while there is nothing wrong with calling it that, because it was the Lord who taught the prayer, it really could be called the Disciples' Prayer. After all, Jesus gave us these words as a prayer for his followers to pray.

Jesus taught his disciples to pray by giving us a model for prayer in Matthew 6, and Christians around the world still use these exact words to pray regularly. We encourage you to pray through these words as a family and memorize them and say them together. Read through the Lord's Prayer in different Bible translations and ask your children to rewrite the prayer in their own words. Take turns praying through the major themes: God's glory, provision for our basic needs, forgiveness, and strength to resist sin. The Lord's Prayer (or Disciples' Prayer) was intended to be a model for our daily prayer.

> Our Father in heaven,
> hallowed be your name.
> Your kingdom come,
> your will be done,
> > on earth as it is in heaven.
> Give us this day our daily bread,
> and forgive us our debts,
> > as we also have forgiven our debtors.
> And lead us not into temptation,
> > but deliver us from evil.
>
> *—Matthew 6:9–13 ESV*

Here are a few ideas of how you can incorporate this prayer into your family prayers. First, focus on God as our Father. It's humbling to start by addressing God in heaven. Spend time praying through God's holiness ("hallowed be your name"), and then open yourselves to his kingdom and will in your family life. Take time to thank God for being the provider for your family. And thank him for giving you the grace to forgive each other as you receive his forgiveness. It's important to recognize that we are in a spiritual battle, so ask God to help you resist temptation and to protect your family from the evil one. As a family, you can structure your prayers on this clear teaching from Jesus himself. What a great gift we have to know exactly how to pray!

# LAUNCH AND LANDING PRAYERS

No matter how busy you are, your family will likely be together during the bookends of the day—first thing in the morning before school or work, and at night before bed. These are ideal times for what we call "launch and landing" prayers.

As the name suggests, a launch prayer gives you a moment to pray for each child, their teachers, their friends, or whatever is needed that day. The landing prayer allows you to close the day well with thanks for the day's blessings. There is a good reason why my wife and I (Jason) get up a little early to have a cup of coffee before the rest of the Housermania crew wakes up. Things get kind of crazy once the kids are out of bed! We usually have a school project to finish, or there are animals to be fed, or homework to stuff into backpacks, cereal to pour, and milk to spill (and hopefully clean up). Our family launches like a bottle rocket on the Fourth of July—a few sparks fly off the short fuse and boom, we lift off.

Somehow, in the midst of all this chaos, either in the kitchen holding hands or in the car on the way to school, we press the pause button long enough to commit our day to Jesus and ask him to lead us. We remind ourselves that we are his and thank him for the day he has given us. We try to start the day according to the encouragement in 1 Thessalonians 5:16–18 to be joyful always, pray continually, and give thanks in all circumstances.

Do we do this perfectly? *No way!* But we do our best to make it a priority, and thankfully, prayer has become part of what we do and who we are as a family.

# PRAY FOR CONVERSION, CHARACTER, AND COURAGE

Prayers for salvation, for growth in godly virtue, and for courage to follow the Lord's direction are just a few of the "big picture" prayers you'll want to say for your children as they grow up. Praying these will help you cultivate a deeper prayer life for your family.

## Conversion

This is the most important prayer that you, as a Christian parent, can pray for your children. Your child's conversion and their decision to place their trust in Jesus will impact them for the rest of eternity. You may see answers to this prayer tomorrow, or it may take twenty years. Of course, your children must make this decision for themselves; you cannot *make* them follow Christ, and no prayer will guarantee their salvation. Still, God listens to our prayers, and he is not deaf to our heartfelt words.

My wife and I (Bobby) prayed earnestly, regularly, and faithfully for our children. Cindy and I believe that this is part of the reason why both of our children were ready to commit their lives to Christ at an early age. My daughter Ashley, for example, would watch me studying the Bible. She also saw me, as a pastor, baptizing different people. So it was natural, at an early age, that she was spiritually aware and curious about her own decision to be baptized. She started asking if she could be baptized when she was seven and continued asking for several months. I told her that trusting and following Jesus was what mattered most, that baptism was secondary. I did not want her to place her focus and hope on the event of baptism without understanding the reason behind it. We had this conversation many times, and I could sense that God was strongly present in her life.

When Ashley turned eight, she brought up getting baptized again. I remember one day she came to me and said, "Dad, you are the one who is making baptism too much of a big deal, because you won't let me do it!" What could I say to her? I guided her to memorize several Bible passages as a foundation for that day, and her mother and I joyfully baptized her. She has not wavered from the faith to this day.

## Character

Another important prayer you will want to pray for your children is to ask God to form their hearts and mold their character. A simple way to pray for this is to repeat or even memorize the apostle Paul's prayer for the Ephesian church. Consider what a difference it would make if you prayed this throughout your children's lives as you went to bed each night: "I bow my knees before the Father, from whom every family in heaven and on earth is named, that according to the riches of his glory he may grant you to be strengthened with power through his Spirit in your inner being, so that Christ may dwell in your hearts through faith—that you, being rooted and grounded in love, may have strength to comprehend with all the saints what is the breadth and length and height and depth, and to know the love of Christ that surpasses knowledge, that you may be filled with all the fullness of God" (Eph. 3:14–19 ESV).

Imagine the blessings that would pour out into your children from your praying this over them.

Praying for character is essential, but it is easily overlooked in our culture today. In the words of Leo Tolstoy, we've become consumed with "particles and progress." We want our children to become the best and the brightest, and our culture naturally focuses on material success, not spiritual success. Ironically, praying for the spirit of a child is the best way to contribute to the ultimate success of a child, in God's eyes.

I (Chad) learned the importance of praying for character when I was in college. Through a series of circumstances, I came to know an upperclassman named Michael DeFazio on a campus visit and asked him if we could get breakfast together early in my freshman year. I wanted some advice on starting out in college, and he highlighted the necessity of prayer. Of all the things he told me to pray for, I remember one of them standing out: "Pray for character." It had never occurred to me to *intentionally pray for and seek after* character, to ask God to mold and shape specific things like this in my life. I just assumed that good character happened over time!

Praying for specific character qualities in your children is something you can start doing right now while they are young.

God hears our prayers and responds. Think about your children and where they need to grow. Then pray for them to grow in joy or humility or boldness, pray for them to develop patience and gratitude, to be kind and generous. Pray specifically for these things and then look for ways to encourage these qualities in your children as God gives opportunities for character development.

## Courage

God wants to mold and shape our character to make us more like Jesus, but the way we live out those character traits according to our unique design and personality will take courage. Ephesians 2:10 says, "We are his workmanship, created in Christ Jesus for good works, which God prepared beforehand, that we should walk in them" (ESV). God's desire is that we will walk in his ways and live out our faith through good works that bless others. But this will take courage, since we live in a fallen, broken world.

Parents need to pray for their children to have courage to grow into their gifting from God. In Romans 12:6–8, Paul describes some of the gifts God gives to Christians: "Having gifts that differ according to the grace given to us, let us use them: if prophecy, in proportion to our faith; if service, in our serving; the one who teaches, in his teaching; the one who exhorts, in his exhortation; the one who contributes, in generosity; the one who leads, with zeal; the one who does acts of mercy, with cheerfulness" (ESV). These gifts are not always as "spiritual" as we often think. They include things like teaching others, showing generosity, and demonstrating acts of mercy.

As parents, we want to help nurture our children so that they live the life God has for them, but we don't always have the wisdom we need. We need God's help to direct us in supporting our children. As stewards of our children's lives, we have a powerful voice, but sadly, many parents don't use that voice to embolden their children to pursue what is good and godly. Pray that God will give you wisdom and boldness to speak into your children's lives as they grow up. Pray that they would be receptive to hearing you, that you would be able to share wisdom from your own experience.

Finally, pray that God would help you see the unique personal gifts he has given your child, so that you can affirm and encourage them. My wife, Heidi, and I (Jason) pray for God to reveal to us the gifts he has placed in each of our kids, so we can help nurture their calling. As we have prayed for the Lord to show us these gifts, we have seen how our daughter has a passion for art. Most children love creative projects, but she has a talent for expressing herself through pictures. We have started framing her art and hanging it in our home and in my office.

Our middle son, Brandon, has always asked profound questions as we talk about the Bible. At the age of six, he was asking questions we didn't have clear answers to. He is able to connect well with people and has a contagious joy about him. He also has a gift for music that we are helping him develop through lessons in our home. Our oldest son, Ben, loves technology, so we encourage him to use his abilities to serve the Lord. He has started serving on the media team at church and video recording the services. As parents, we want to help prepare our kids for what the Lord has created them to do, so they can develop their gifts and learn how to use them to serve others. That's why we pray that God would reveal to us the unique gifts he has given our kids, so we can encourage them and help them grow into mature believers who confidently live out their faith.

# CONCLUSION

Cecil and Levine Bailey served as missionaries in India and teachers at a Christian school in western Canada. Canada has a religiously hostile, secular culture, yet all of their children and grandchildren have made decisions to follow Jesus. My wife, Cindy, and I (Bobby) took a trip with the elderly Baileys to a Christian conference in another province. The Baileys stopped to get gas and supplies halfway through the trip, and when Levine got out of the car and slipped into the store, I took the opportunity to ask Cecil a few questions about his family.

"Cecil," I asked, "what is the key to raising children to faithfully follow Jesus?"

"Well, you know," he said, "Levine was always talking to the kids about God, taking them to church, and praying for them."

A few minutes later the group again separated to do some shopping, and I had a moment alone with Levine, so I asked her the same question. "Levine," I said, "let me ask you for some advice. What do you think is the key to raising children who faithfully follow Jesus?"

"Well, I have to credit Cecil," she replied. "He always emphasized the importance of church and prayed for all our kids so faithfully. It's really because of Cecil."

Several months afterward, I had the joy of dropping in on a party at our church where the Baileys' extended family celebrated the couple's fiftieth wedding anniversary. As I was walking down the hall toward the room, I could hear their five kids and dozens of their grandchildren all rejoicing and singing hymns together. *Who does that?* I thought.

I don't think there was any secret formula that Cecil and Levine Bailey followed. They weren't unique in their parenting. They were not spiritual giants with a secret. They simply prayed faithfully for their children and grandchildren and faithfully followed the Lord in their lives. Be encouraged! Today you can begin creating the same kind of legacy in your own family.

# DEDICATION IN ACTION

REMEMBER. Recall Jesus' prayer for his disciples in John 17.

- Pray, knowing that your children are a gift from God.
- Pray for their protection in the midst of a hostile world.
- Pray for their dedication to God.

CONSIDER. What can you do to cultivate a life of prayer? Consider how you can pray as an individual, as a couple, as a family, and with friends.

PRAY. Ask the Lord to give you a greater desire to pray than you already have, and pray for your children's conversion, pray for their character, and pray that God will give them the courage to pursue his direction in life.

RESPOND. How is the Holy Spirit leading you *today* to live out your dedication to God in prayer?

LISTEN. "Be Joyful Always" (1 Thess. 5:16–18), *Seeds of Purpose*, Seeds Family Worship.

# CHAPTER 8

# DEDICATED TO DISCIPLINE

"MY SON, DO NOT DESPISE the LORD's discipline or be weary of his reproof, for the LORD reproves him whom he loves, as a father the son in whom he delights" (Prov. 3:11–12 ESV). The topic of disciplining children is controversial in our culture today. Even in the church, there are a variety of perspectives and views on the subject. But despite the disagreement among parents and church leaders, most everyone agrees that some form of discipline is necessary when raising children. In fact, the word *discipleship* shares the same root word as *discipline*, and the two are closely related. Becoming a disciple of Jesus takes discipline.

One of the key lessons we have discovered is that the Lord shapes us into the image of Christ through parenting. Parenting is not easy! There are struggles, disappointments, and failures. And as we disciple our children (and others in the family of God), God uses our efforts and mistakes to disciple us as well. In fact, his discipline in our lives is one of the primary ways he disciples us.

When our children (Jason) were young, my wife and I took part in a parenting class at our church called "Effective Parenting in a Defective World."[1] Author Chip Ingram thoughtfully led us through some of the roadblocks and land mines that parents must learn to navigate as they discipline their children. His teaching helped us grasp the biblical perspective on discipline that we've just mentioned. He also addressed the reality that many parents have experienced terrible abuse in their childhood, and this makes disciplining their own children a difficult issue. Some have a hard time even talking about it, let alone practicing it.

One of the greatest blessings we took away from these teaching sessions was Chip's definition of discipline. It has dramatically impacted the way we have raised our kids. Over and over again, he reminded us:

The goal of biblical discipline is discipleship.

The goal is discipleship, and discipleship for dedicated parents is training your children to trust and follow Jesus. He encouraged parents to think about discipline *as* discipleship rather than punishment.

This connects to a truth from God's Word. In Ephesians 6:4, the apostle Paul tells fathers, "Do not exasperate your children; instead, bring them up in the training and instruction of the Lord." The goal of godly discipline is not to crush the spirit of a child, to shame the child into obedience. It is to lovingly teach them what is right and good and to lead them to the Savior who can rescue them from their sin. As parents, we've tried to use moments of correction as opportunities to teach our children God's ways.

Of course, none of this is easy or simple. Even knowing that the goal of discipline is discipleship, we'll be the first to admit that we still struggle as parents to find the balance between being too strict and being too passive. And as we said earlier when we discussed the practice of family worship, we want to emphasize that there is no one-size-fits-all approach to administering discipline.

In the sections that follow, we won't be able to fully address this issue and answer every question or explore every method. We want to highlight that discipline is necessary—a biblical nonnegotiable—and that as a parent, you need to seek the Lord as you consider how to discipline your children. Rather than prescribing methods of discipline (time-outs, spanking, and so on), we have included several examples in our stories and illustrations, but the particular methods will vary from family to family.

## THE HEART OF GODLY DISCIPLINE

The wisdom writer of Proverbs 3:11–12 encourages us as God's children not to fight against the discipline of the Lord but to trust in the greater work he is doing. The writer of Hebrews 12:5–11 (ESV) picks up on this theme.

> Have you forgotten the exhortation that addresses you as sons?
>
> *"My son, do not regard lightly the discipline of the Lord,*
> *nor be weary when reproved by him.*
> *For the Lord disciplines the one he loves,*
> *and chastises every son whom he receives."*
>
> It is for discipline that you have to endure. God is treating you as sons. For what son is there whom his father does not discipline? If you are left without discipline, in which all have participated, then you are illegitimate children and not sons. Besides this, we have had earthly fathers who disciplined us and we respected them. Shall we not much more be subject to the Father of spirits and live? For they disciplined us for a short time as it seemed best to them, but he disciplines us for our good, that we may share his holiness. For the moment all discipline seems painful rather than pleasant, but later it yields the peaceful fruit of righteousness to those who have been trained by it.

This text exhorts Christians not to let their hearts grow weary as God walks them through seasons of discipline. It places discipline in the context of relationship. When God disciplines us, he does so not as a judge, punishing us for breaking the law, but as a loving Father who wants to see us grow into mature children who share in his holiness. This passage highlights that our Father is working for the ultimate good of his children.

At the same time, these verses also give us a powerful vision for parenting our children. They serve as an illustration of why we need to have loving discipline in our home. God, as our Father, disciplines us as his children, and this models for us how we discipline our own children. We know many parents who are tempted to give up on discipline, either because they were not disciplined themselves or because their parents were too harsh in their discipline. The key to godly discipline is understanding the goal of discipline—to train your children to trust and follow Jesus. We discipline our children for the same reason God disciplines us—for their good, that they would grow in holiness and become more like Jesus. And we do it out of love for them, knowing that this is what is truly best for them. Regardless of what you think about the methods of disciplining children, we can all agree on these goals. So don't give up. Even if discipline is hard, it is necessary.

The passage begins by laying the foundation that discipline is important, and it reminds us that discipline is not meant to be discouraging. Discipline should encourage believers, because the Lord disciplines the children he delights in and loves. This is the heart of godly discipline. Love must encompass every aspect of the discipleship process. Our objective is not to discourage our children but to teach them God's best.

We have found that some of the best opportunities we have to train our children come in the midst of disciplining them for the most trying acts of disobedience. In these moments, it is critical that we have the biblical vision for discipline clearly in our mind so we are able to respond to these situations in love, rather than reacting in frustration and anger. As parents, we want to make sure we instruct our children out of our love for them and because we want God's best in their lives, not because we are irritated and tired. Sometimes we just need to take a moment to stop and think, to calm down, before we engage in discipline. This isn't easy, but it's a great habit to form!

Verses 7–9 tell us that the Lord disciplines all of his children—no exceptions. This means that discipline is necessary for all of us who trust and follow Jesus. The verses go on to say that earthly fathers discipline their children, and their children *respect* them for it. Notice that the Scriptures connect the practice of intentional, loving discipline with respect. Consistent, if imperfect, instruction will create healthy boundaries for children and establish an environment in which they feel safe. In his commentary on Hebrews, John MacArthur writes, "It is the disciplined child who respects their parents. The surest way for a parent to lose, or never gain, his child's respect is to never correct or punish him, no matter how terrible the child's behavior. Even while they are growing up, children instinctively know that a parent who disciplines fairly is a parent who loves and cares."[2]

## THE GOAL OF GODLY DISCIPLINE

As we mentioned earlier, discipline has a specific purpose for Christians: holiness. Verse 10 says that the Lord "disciplines us for our good, that we may share his holiness" (ESV). Since God's purpose in discipline is to develop holiness in us, parents can partner with God as they too work to cultivate a holy life in their children through discipline. This long-term goal in discipline is infinitely more important than the short-term goals that parents are often tempted to focus on. Frequently, parents sacrifice teaching and instructing their children just to get a child to be quiet, resorting to shouting or threatening them. Some parents bribe their children into obedience, while others discipline in anger and create fear and resentment in their relationship with their kids. The objective of discipline is long-term: to teach children obedience and forge strong character rooted in an accurate understanding of the gospel of God's grace. To put it simply, we want our children to know Christ and to follow him from the heart, to be his disciples.

Verse 11 acknowledges something we can all agree on: "all discipline seems painful rather than pleasant" (ESV). No one enjoys receiving discipline. But that doesn't change the need for it. Discipline will always seem painful to the child, but that momentary pain, inflicted for their benefit, could end up saving them from a lifetime of pain and suffering.

We also want to point out that discipline is painful for both the parents and the children. Often, despite our best efforts, children do not fully understand why we are disciplining them. It is frequently much more painful for the parents as they are walking their children through these times of correction. The cliche "this is going to hurt me more than it hurts you" usually proves to be true, even if kids never believe it. Dedicated parents must learn to commit to the discipline process and trust that the Lord is with them as they seek to practice this in raising their children according to God's Word.

Discipline, as an aspect of discipleship, is more of a process than an event. The last thing I (Jason) want to hear from my wife as I walk through the door at the end of a hard day are these words: "We have a situation. You need to deal with it." But it happens. I remember one evening when one of our sons was seven. I had given him a pocketknife, thinking he was ready to handle that kind of responsibility (in my defense, it was a very small knife). I even gave him explicit instructions, telling him that if he abused this privilege in any way, the knife would immediately be taken away from him.

For several months, there were no problems. Then my wife found that the headrest of the leather seat in the back of her van had been "wounded." We asked our son if he had used his knife to cut the seat, but he adamantly denied the charge. He almost had us convinced that it might have been someone else. We brought in some CSI forensics experts, took fingerprints, and interrogated all of his friends under a hot light at our kitchen table. Maybe that's a bit of an exaggeration, but we did do a bit of detective work. We deduced that the new pocketknife was indeed the weapon used in the crime.

When we confronted him a second time, he broke. Tears flowed as we talked to him in his room. We left him there for a few minutes so we could discuss our plan for discipline. And we needed a little time to cool down. As upset as we were that he had destroyed the headrest, we were more concerned about his lying to us. We had experienced a couple other times when he had lied, and we knew that this needed to be corrected, for his benefit and for the good of our family. We decided that the best option was to give him a spanking and walk him through a process of reconciliation.

We went back into his room and talked through his actions. We shared with him how his lies had hurt everyone in our family because they had destroyed our trust. We explained that lying is a sin, and because of his sin, he had disobeyed God and dishonored us, his parents. We asked him if he wanted to ask God and us for forgiveness. He said yes, and we led him through a prayer asking God for forgiveness. We told him that we forgave him too.

Then we informed him that he was going to be spanked for his disobedience. After I spanked him, I hugged him and told him I loved him. I reminded him that a father disciplines a child he loves, and that was why I was doing this. We left him alone in his room and asked him to let us know when he was ready to come back and join the family.

He stayed in his room for at least thirty minutes and then asked to join us. We reassured him that we were glad he was back with us, and we continued on with our night. We didn't mention it to him again. As difficult as it is for us to follow through in times like these, we knew it was the right thing.

There are a few things I'd like to highlight from this example with our son. First, if you haven't experienced this already, you will soon. When a child is disobedient, it is difficult to remain calm. Most parents get angry with their children at some point, and the flesh—the sinful nature in all of us—reacts selfishly rather than responding in love. In these moments, a parent needs to regain composure, pray, and step back from the situation before disciplining the child.

You'll also notice that we addressed our son directly and told him specifically *how* he had been disobedient, in words appropriate to his age level. We reminded him that we loved him, and we made sure he understood that we were disciplining him because we wanted what was best for him. We took the time to walk him through the process of forgiveness, both with us and with the Lord. All of this took a significant amount of time and energy, but it's critical to the discipline process. After this, I administered the appropriate discipline that my wife and I had decided on, and we both hugged him and reassured him of our love for him. Finally, we left him in his room to give him some time to think about his disobedience and consider the consequences. This gave him a chance to calm down, to let his emotions settle, and to reflect and learn from what he had just experienced. We made sure he knew that he was free to rejoin the family when he was ready; the discipline was over.

## THE HARVEST OF GODLY DISCIPLINE

At the end of the passage we've been studying in the book of Hebrews, there is an amazing word of encouragement. God promises us that if we are willing to walk through the hard process of discipline, there is a wonderful result: "For the moment all discipline seems painful rather than pleasant, but later it *yields the peaceful fruit of righteousness* to those who have been trained by it" (v. 11, emphasis added).

A farmer has to wait months before his crops are ready for harvest. Whether we're talking about apples or oranges, growth doesn't happen overnight. But today we live in a culture of instant gratification. We lack the patience to wait for things that develop over time, preferring immediate results. The harvest of discipline doesn't come immediately after we administer correction to our children. It takes time. You may not see the fruit until tomorrow, a year from now, or even ten years from now. That's why you'll need to have faith in God and his promises. You'll need to believe that the result God promises is better, in the long run, than any immediate results you can gain from other ways of responding to your kids.

BOBBY: Children naturally press boundaries, and they need to know there are certain violations parents will not tolerate. Because I grew up in a home with a lot of sibling rivalry, my wife and I were determined to train our children to get along with each other. We wanted a peaceful home.

Ashley and Chad loved to play together, but it often led to disagreements. So Cindy developed a great method of discipline, which helped lead to peace in our home. Sometimes Ashley and Chad would fight and come to her with two different versions of what had happened. Cindy would lead them to a room and tell them that she was going to close the door and that they were not allowed out until they both agreed on what had happened. Only one story was allowed!

This practice forced them to talk through their disagreements and work things out. Sometimes it would take them a long time, but they *had* to come up with a mutually agreeable story. When they did that, the conflict would often be resolved quickly.

But there is an added blessing in this! You see, God is also cultivating patience in your life, one of the fruits of his Spirit. And trust us, you will need it.

You will also see the benefit of discipline as God's character grows in your children. You will be leading them to the Lord, helping them understand their sin and their need for a Savior. You will be cultivating the soil of their heart and planting the seeds of godly character by teaching and modeling the gospel to them. It may take several years for these seeds to bear fruit, but God is faithful!

As a toddler, my (Jason) niece, Kylie, would have made James Dobson's "strong-willed child" top ten list. She created chaos in her parents' lives. One time, she finger-painted an entire wall while her parents were in another room. They were a young couple, and she was their first child, and she was determined to prove that she was in charge. Kylie always wanted to have things her way, and if that didn't happen, she would clear the room with an epic meltdown. Her parents were desperate for peace, so they sought wise biblical counsel and developed a plan to discipline their daughter. They faithfully discipled her through discipline, and eventually she came to understand and submit to their authority.

Today Kylie is one of the most joy-filled followers of Jesus I know. She is fourteen years old and is walking with the Lord and trusting him. She has an infectious smile, and she reflects the goodness of Christ in such a beautiful way. The Lord has put a special fire and passion in her spirit, and she knows that it is best expressed under the authority of her parents. I believe that the Lord has gifted her to lead others, but her stubbornness and rebelliousness needed to be reshaped—changed from selfishness to the meekness of Christ—to make her more like Jesus. Every time I go to Joshua and Linda's home now, I feel the peace of the Lord. Their home is a great reminder to me that God faithfully produces a harvest as we plant the seeds of godly character in the hearts of our children. It encourages me to be faithful as I work through the unpleasant aspects of discipline in order to enjoy the harvest of righteousness.

Discipline is a challenge, but it is vital. And godly discipline is a combination of love, wisdom, and consequences. We are best at disciplining our children when we reflect our Father's loving heart and his desire for holiness. Most people tend to think of God as overly lenient or overly strict. But God is neither of these. In Romans 11:22, Paul describes how God's holy love can be expressed in different ways—as kindness or as severity, depending on the situation: "Note then the kindness and the severity of God: severity toward those who have fallen, but God's kindness to you, provided you continue in his kindness. Otherwise you too will be cut off" (ESV).

As Christian parents, you will need to exercise wisdom to practice discipline in a balanced way that reflects the discipline of God. Sometimes you will need to emphasize the severe consequences of rebellion; at other times you'll need to highlight the kindness and mercy of God. In every situation, you must learn to point your children to the grace of God, showing them that like your discipline of them, God's discipline is for their own good, to help them become more like Jesus.

There is one additional important principle in training our children that is often neglected today. It is the foundation of discipline. We are talking about children showing their parents honor and respect.

## HONORING YOUR FATHER AND YOUR MOTHER

According to the Bible, certain people and positions should receive more respect and honor than should others. This applies especially to parents. Ephesians 6:1–3 says, "Children, obey your parents in the Lord, for this is right. 'Honor your father and mother' (this is the first commandment with a promise), 'that it may go well with you and that you may live long in the land'" (ESV). This comes from the Ten Commandments (Exod. 20:12), so we know it's very important. It's not just a good parenting technique or a traditional value; it's a core biblical command from God.

Many cultural beliefs do not match up with this biblical teaching on honor. Here are some common ideas that are inconsistent with what the Bible teaches.

- Honor is only to be given if the parent is perceived as earning it.
- Honor is only to be given if it "feels right."
- Honor is only to be given if the parent reciprocates.

Honoring your father and mother is respecting their position as parents, whether or not it feels right, whether or not they reciprocate. Honor is based on the design of the family as God established it.

When children honor their father and mother, they "hold them as weighty" (the basic meaning of the Hebrew verb translated as "honor"). This means that children who live in the home are to respect and obey their parents. The principle of honoring parents carries over into adulthood, when children are responsible to take care of their parents, if needed, in their parents' old age (1 Tim. 5:3–8).

So create a culture of respect in the home. This means that your children obey you, speak respectfully to you, and treat you as weighty and revered. And continue to teach them to respect you, especially as they reach adolescence and are influenced by cultural ideas contrary to this teaching. Remember, blessing comes with obedience to this command.

When parents teach their children to show them respect, even as they discipline their children, they are teaching them to respect

God. If your children learn to honor imperfect parents in the home, they will be set up to honor and obey their perfect heavenly Father long after they leave home.

## DEDICATION IN ACTION

REMEMBER. Memorize Proverbs 3:11–12 as a family.

> My son, do not despise the LORD's discipline or be weary of his reproof; for the LORD reproves him whom he loves, as a father the son in whom he delights. (ESV)

CONSIDER. What can you apply to your parenting from the way God has disciplined you throughout your life? Think about how you have seen God working on you to produce righteousness as described in Hebrews 12:7–11.

PRAY. Ask God for insight on how to discipline your children appropriately so they will live in peace instead of chaos.

RESPOND. How is the Holy Spirit leading you *today* to live out your dedication to God in disciplining your children?

LISTEN. "Children and Fathers" (Eph. 6:4), *Seeds of Character*, Seeds Family Worship.

# CHAPTER 9

# DEDICATED TO THE CHURCH

**LIFE IS BUSY.** We have so many commitments—work, school, taking care of the house, and endless sports activities. For many people today, church seems like more trouble than it's worth. And sadly, more and more Christians in North America are questioning their involvement in the local church. But God's Word is clear: we need to be actively involved in the church, connected relationally with other believers. This is especially true for families seeking to raise and train their kids in the Lord. But why is the church so important for families? Here are a few questions to consider.

- Do you believe that the church is central to God's plan to transform humanity?
- If you aren't involved in a local church, how will you honor and follow the passages in the Bible that speak of our need to relate to one another in relationship as we grow to maturity together in Christ?
- Where else will you, as a parent, learn about Jesus and learn to disciple your children in the ways of Jesus?

- Where will your children turn to for help in growing as a disciple of Jesus when they reach adulthood?

God gave us the local church as the foundation and pillar of truth in a lost and spiritually darkened world (1 Tim. 3:15). The church is God's plan A for how he transforms the world with the gospel of Jesus. He intended that the church would reveal his wisdom to the world (Eph. 3:10). As followers of Jesus, we are the guardians of his message for the world, and we are called to be a community that lives out the words of Jesus. We are a light to the world. Without the church, it is impossible to obey many of the passages we read in the Bible. Trusting and following Jesus has never been something disciples can faithfully live and practice alone.

In the church, parents learn how to follow Jesus. They learn how to disciple their children. Families build relationships with other families, and they follow Jesus together. Children and teens form relationships with others who will support them and encourage them to live for God's kingdom, and they find support for their faith when they leave home and go out into the world as adults.

North Americans tend to be individualistic, focusing on what is best for them and what meets their needs, but that's not what we see in the Bible. God's plan isn't just about fulfilling our individual desires; it's focused on what God wants to do with his people as a community, his family. The local church is the fundamental manifestation of God's kingdom on earth, and God's ultimate plan is to equip people to trust and follow Jesus and grow to maturity as disciples *in the church*.

In our society, we often compartmentalize our lives into fragmented pieces, keeping them distinct from each other. We go to work, go to the gym, go to classes, spend time at home, and attend sporting events. The temptation to compartmentalize our lives is especially strong when it comes to church. *We go to church,* we tell ourselves, *but it's hard to connect with God and with others.* And it's true! It's not always easy to develop relationships with others if you see them for only an hour once a week. Still, we know that God designed Christian families to be connected in a church, and this is a key component of dedicated, spiritual parenting. But it will take work to make it happen.

The American mindset has taught us how to live on our own, isolated from others. We believe that we don't need anyone else to be sufficient or successful, and we think that's a good thing! But the American dream does not align with God's dream for his children. He has designed our families to function best within a broader community of faith. As in the African proverb "It takes a village to raise a child," we argue that it takes a church to raise a child to be a fully committed, mature follower of Christ.

CHAD: When I was young and our family planted Harpeth Community Church, I joined the set-up team, which included several men from the church. We arrived early at the local elementary school, where we met each Sunday at 7:00 a.m. These guys were awesome, and these early mornings taught me many things about setting up a stage and sound system, showing up on time, and how Murphy's Law applies to church planting. But more than this, I experienced what it means to belong to the body of Christ. The people there cared enough about the church to show up three hours early to get the gymnasium ready for an encounter with God.

The older I get, the more I see what an amazing gift God has given us in the church. Today I can proudly say (as a pastor's kid) that I love the church, because the church is my extended family. Because I'm a part of the church, I belong to something bigger than myself.

The body of Christ, in all her diversity of gifts and callings, has much to offer your children as they grow in faith. And you have the responsibility of introducing them into that community and teaching them what it means to belong to God's people.

The ancient writer Aristotle was not a Christian, but he helpfully outlined the key elements of a successful society. The first building block of any society, he said, is the family unit.[1] A nation is not just a collection of individuals; it is a network of interconnected families. While this view isn't as common today in our individualistic culture, it is far closer to the biblical view of society. And this perspective is particularly relevant for parents today. Because the family is a central part of shaping society, this means that God's kingdom is at work, powerfully, in our homes.

Discipleship begins in the home, but it doesn't end there. The work that parents invest in discipling their children will one day influence who they are as adults in the world. And the church is the community that God has provided for families to turn to for encouragement, guidance, and accountability. So let's take a journey and rediscover the riches of God's grace in his community of faith. If you are not currently involved in a church community, you may be surprised by how much the church can help you in your work as a parent.

My (Jason) family has experienced firsthand the power of the local church. When my wife and I were young parents, Harpeth Community Church, where my coauthor Bobby Harrington pastors, played a critical role in the Lord's work in redeeming and restoring our struggling marriage. Church leaders walked with us through those storms and eventually directed us to discern God's calling in our lives, leading to the birth of the Seeds Family Worship ministry at a vacation Bible school.

Bobby and the elders saw what the Lord was doing through our VBS work and prayerfully decided to start a new kind of service to minister to the families at our church. I still recall leaving a prayer meeting with our church planning team after we first discussed the idea of a service for families. Bobby put his arm around my shoulders (which felt a little bit like a headlock at the time) and told me he believed the Lord was leading us in this new direction. He asked me to put together a proposal to present to the elder board. I was hesitant, but Bobby encouraged me to trust the Lord's leading and take the next step.

We met with the elders and they affirmed the idea, so I scheduled a follow-up meeting with Bobby to ask how he wanted the service to be structured. To my surprise, there were few specifics. He told me to use the gifts God had given me and just do it. At the time, it sounded to my ears like he was giving me enough

BOBBY: After we began the family service, for the next few years Jason and I would meet and talk about music and family ministry. His music was being widely used by the families in our church, and he had begun reaching a broader audience. When I would teach about parents discipling their children, I would use Jason and Heidi as examples. At this time, we also started holding "children's days" at our church. These were special days when the focus was on training our children to trust and follow Jesus, and Jason would lead the praise and worship for us. The church loved these events.

Over time, God continued to bless Jason's ministry, and under God's leadership, he joined our staff and started leading a family worship experience every week. Jason was on staff at the church for about a year before he and his family moved back to Idaho to be near their extended family. Since that time, Seeds Family Worship has grown and expanded into a national ministry. Discipling Jason and his wife, Heidi, has been one of the greatest joys of my life, and I'm excited to see where God will take the ministry he has started through them.

rope to hang myself, but looking back, I see that he was growing me up in the Lord. I was being discipled to be a leader, learning how to follow God's leading and take action, and God was doing a new work in beginning a unique service to build up families in our church.

In many ways, this was the genesis of the book you are now reading. The insights here grow out of the wisdom we learned at our church, and through Bobby's teaching and the example he and his wife have shown as parents. Looking back on this journey, I can see how God used the broken chapters of my family's story to serve his people, the church. He brought life out of the ashes of my struggling marriage and gave me a new purpose and calling. God uses our relationships in the church to speak his truth and his vision into our lives. We need the church in order for us to grow as disciples of Jesus, and to help our children grow and mature as well.

## WHY CHURCH?

While we tend to think of our faith as a matter that's just between *God and me*, the Bible repeatedly says that it's really about *God and us*. God's plan is that we follow Jesus in community with others. In case you doubt that this is what the Bible teaches, we thought it might be helpful to you if we summarized the case for the church.[2]

There are three primary reasons why the church is necessary, particularly for families.

1. To obey God
2. To serve God
3. To reveal God

An in-depth study of the New Testament would yield a great deal of insight about each of these, but we want to keep it simple, so we'll focus on just one passage for each reason.

## To Obey God

The first reason why we should belong to a church is because it's a matter of obedience to God's commandment. Consider what is written to the church in the letter to the Hebrews. These were disciples of Jesus who were struggling with their faith, and some of them had stopped meeting with the church. They were trying to do it alone, thinking, *Who needs the church?* In response, the writer of Hebrews had this to say to them: "Let us hold fast the confession of our hope without wavering, for he who promised is faithful. And let us consider how to stir up one another to love and good works, not neglecting to meet together, as is the habit of some, but encouraging one another, and all the more as you see the Day drawing near" (Heb. 10:23–25 ESV).

The word to these struggling believers is clear: they should not neglect meeting together. Why? Because each of us has a need for support and encouragement *in order to "hold fast the confession of our hope without wavering"* (v. 23, emphasis added). Discipleship is difficult, and meeting with other believers helps us to spur one another on to love and good works. The church is where we encourage each other with the truth that Jesus is coming back for us.

## To Serve God

The second reason why we need the church is because it is the primary arena where we are to serve and use the gifts God has given us. God has given us all responsibilities in the local church. A simple passage teaching this concept is Romans 12:4–5. Notice what Paul says here. He tells us that each of us — regular, everyday Christians — is a part of the body of Christ (the church), and we are members of each other. We belong to one another. "As in one body we have many members, and the members do not all have the same function, so we, though many, are one body in Christ, and individually members one of another" (ESV).

Each Christian belongs to the other Christians in the local church. As a part of the body, we all have gifts and abilities, and God teaches us that we must use them in his church: "As each has received a gift, use it to serve one another, as good stewards of God's varied grace: whoever speaks, as one who speaks oracles of God; whoever serves, as one who serves by the strength that God supplies—in order that in everything God may be glorified through Jesus Christ" (1 Peter 4:10–11 ESV).

How can we do this if we are not active in the church? The only way we can fulfill these teachings is to be functioning as a part of the church body (see also 1 Cor. 12:13–29; Eph. 4:11–16).

## To Reveal God

The third reason why we need to belong to a church is because God intends for the church to be a picture of the gospel, a means of revealing himself to the world. God wants Christians to be a part of the church because in the church, we reveal what God has done through Jesus. The church shows the world what it means to be a redeemed people who demonstrate and live out God's wisdom. The church even reveals God's wisdom to the spiritual forces in the heavenly realms. Paul describes this in Ephesians 3:7–10: "Grace was given [to me] ... to bring to light for everyone what is the plan of the mystery hidden for ages in God who created all things, so that through the church the manifold wisdom of God might now be made known to the rulers and authorities in the heavenly places" (ESV). In other words, God's plan is to make his wisdom known *through the church*. Throughout the New Testament, we learn that God's plan is to reveal himself through the church, and he wants all believers to be involved in that plan.

◆　◆　◆

These three reasons summarize a large body of teaching in the New Testament, and there are hundreds of passages supporting what we've talked about here. A person who chooses to opt out of the local church isn't just making a casual decision. He or she is opting out of the normal Christian life, the primary means that God has given us for growth into spiritual maturity. Dedication to a local church is presumed and taught in the Bible. Only by being a part of the church can we fully receive and give encouragement, uphold God's plan, and do our part for the church's kingdom mission.

Clearly, God intended his children to partner together in living the Christian life, and to do so within a community. We attend church because it helps us obey God. And if we truly want our children to be kingdom seekers and Christ followers, this will happen only if we are connected to a church. Bottom line: it is difficult to lead children to trust and follow Jesus without involvement in his church family. This means that discipling your children necessarily involves being dedicated to the church.

I (Jason) will admit that this wasn't something I really understood when I first came to know Christ. I didn't grow up in a home that was connected to a church community.

When I was a teenager, a friend from school invited me to attend a church camp in the Sawtooth Mountains in Idaho.

Miraculously, the Lord drew me to himself that week, and I became a Christian. My cabin counselor, Eddie, was very instrumental in this process. I now realize what a sacrifice it was for him to take a week of his vacation time to suffer through sleep deprivation and lead a group of junior high boys at camp. (And if sleep deprivation doesn't get to you, the smell surely will!)

Throughout that week, Eddie introduced me to what "the church" is called to be. He encouraged me as I read the Bible, and he answered my questions well into the night. He saw my hand go up on Thursday evening during the invitation to commit to the Lord, and he came and shared in the excitement and joy as I decided to follow Jesus. Best of all, when we returned from camp, he connected me to a church family. He and his wife, Julie, faithfully led a discipleship group of teens and taught us what it means to follow Jesus. This was my first picture of what church community is supposed to look like, and it was beautiful—exactly what I needed in order to grow as a follower of Jesus.

## HOW TO HELP KIDS GROW IN CHURCH

If you want to make sure your kids stay connected in church, or get them connected for the first time, you will need to make some tough decisions. First and foremost, you must dedicate yourself to being involved in a church. You knew we'd come back to this, didn't you? As we've been saying throughout this book, the first step in discipling your kids is to evaluate your own spiritual life. Are you committed to a church? Do you encourage church involvement in your family? How do you talk about the church to your kids? If you aren't committed, your children aren't likely to be either. They will see what you do and follow your lead, so it's essential that you set a good example for them in this area.

We have heard people claim that family is more important than church. They will tell us, "We need to use Sunday mornings for our family time" or "Our family time is much more significant than attending church, where we're not together." While family time is good and important, this perspective wrongly assumes there must be a conflict between family time and church attendance. It's not an either/or; it's a both/and. Look at your priorities and designate another time each week for your family to be together. Dedicate Sunday mornings (or Saturday evenings) for involvement in the church.

We understand that you may be too busy to set apart an entire evening for your family during the week, but that's a problem that can be fixed over time. We must learn to make sacrifices of time if our relationship with our kids really comes first. Get out your schedule, look at your commitments, and decide what needs to be dropped. But we suggest that involvement in church should be the *last* thing you remove from the schedule. In his book *Stop Dating the Church*, pastor Josh Harris writes, "The church is earth's single best place—God's specially designed place—to start over, to grow and to change for the glory of God. That's why I tell people that when they stop dating the church, they're not just adding another item to a long spiritual to-do list. Instead, they're getting started on experiencing all the other blessings that Jesus promised to his followers as the fruits of the truly abundant life."[3]

For your children to become more like Christ, they must be connected to the larger family of spiritual brothers and sisters, not just to your family. So we must learn to make *both* relationships a priority. The stakes are high when it comes to the way we handle church involvement, because God has chosen the church as the context for discipleship, even though families have the primary responsibility for discipling their kids.

In the book *You Lost Me*—a look at why young people are leaving the faith—David Kinnaman describes twentysomethings who drop out of the faith. Most twentysomethings, he concludes, "are not walking away from faith, they are putting involvement in church on hold."[4] They are not leaving forever, just for a season of fun. He finishes, saying, "Most young Christians are struggling less with their faith in Christ than with their experience of church."[5] We see this as a call to parents and to churches, not to make church more relevant but to make faith real as it is taught and lived out in the church. Twentysomethings who are seeking God, in our experience, are not looking for the best show in town. They want authentic faith communities in which people practice what they preach and visibly display the grace of the gospel to one another and to the world.

Perhaps you've had some bad experiences with the church in the past. We understand. Churches are filled with broken people who still sin and hurt others. But don't let that experience keep you from obedience to God. The Bible tells us that being a part of a healthy church matters for the long-term sustainability of faith, and this will be especially true for your children when they leave home. Start teaching church faithfulness now. It begins with your dedication, and it will develop in your kids over time.

# CHURCH COMMITMENTS FOR DEDICATED PARENTS

*1. I Will Continue to Value It When My Kids Don't.* As your kids enter the middle school and high school years, they will begin making important decisions about life. They will face choices about alcohol, drugs, dating relationships, and sexual temptation. They will have greater freedom and will be making more choices about their future than ever before, and they will need a strong connection to church. The influence of Christian friends can make all the difference in the world.

You *will* get pushback from your kids on this, but as a wise mother once said, "Any child worth his salt is going to fight you about church involvement." From the moment they're born, our kids begin pushing for their independence, and that is a good, healthy part of their development. After all, they will eventually be on their own, without our guidance and oversight. As parents, we need to encourage this growing self-sufficiency without compromising faithfulness to the church.

We've seen many parents who have good intentions and don't want their kids to "hate" church refrain from compelling church involvement. They make attendance at church optional. But what does this communicate about the value and importance of church? After all, we require our children to go to school, brush their teeth, and get to bed on time. We make them do many things for their long-term benefit, whether they want to or not. Doesn't church fall into this category? It is something we do to benefit our children spiritually in the long run. As parents, we want to teach our kids self-discipline and give them the best possible chance at life. If we insist on these other activities, why not insist on church?

Sometimes our kids protest that they "don't get anything out of church." Our response is that church is not just about what we get out of it as individuals; it's more about what God is doing in the church as a whole. Jesus came to serve, and that is our attitude as well. Model this approach in your life and make it a priority to serve others in your local church.

I (Bobby) understand that this requires making some difficult choices. When our family lived in Canada, our son, Chad—like every other boy in the country—wanted to play hockey. But to be a good hockey player in Canada, you must give up much of your life to practices, scrimmages, and games. And many of the games are played on Sunday morning.

We allowed him to play, but we had a rule: no hockey on Sunday morning. The one exception to this rule was a playoff game, because they weren't a regular occurrence and we realized that our son's absence would let down his team at a crucial time. The coach tried to change my mind about several games during the season, but we held fast and refused to let Chad play on Sundays, so he could go to church with us. For the playoff game, I attended church with Chad on Sunday night so he could play that Sunday morning.

Years later, we moved to Tennessee and planted the church where I now pastor. Our daughter, Ashley, was thirteen at the time, a difficult age for any girl and a traumatic time for such a big move. We *insisted* that she attend youth group on Sunday nights, and one Sunday evening this became a major battle in our home. After fighting about it, Ashley went to church, and when she returned home, I asked her how it went. "No one else showed up," she said. "It was just me and the youth minister." Her faithfulness, her obedience, and her disappointment broke my heart. But over the long haul, God has given our children a love for the church. Ashley is now in her thirties, and she mentors high school girls as part of the Celebrate Recovery ministry in our church.

Some parents choose to send their children to a Christian school, but even if your kids attend one, don't substitute that for the church. The type of school a child attends (whether public, private, or home school) is not the biggest predictor of a child's faith. What makes the difference is the example of parents who disciple at home and are active in the church. Even if your children are surrounded by Christian peers at school, they will need the support and encouragement of a youth group. They also need to be worshiping regularly with other families at weekend services.

And let's not forget something else in all this: the church needs them! Christian education can be important, but regardless of where your child goes to school, involvement in church sets the pattern for their adult years, when Christian high school will be just a memory. Your child's regular participation also encourages other teens in the church, many of whom do not have the advantages of a Christian school environment.

*2. I Will Connect My Kids with Other Kids at Church.* One way to begin building a positive attitude toward church is to help your children form relationships with other kids in their age group. This can start at a very early age. Consistency in attending Sunday school, even when children are just a year or two old, can help them develop good feelings about church. And you'd be surprised by how much they learn.

We (Bobby and Cindy) cultivated relationships with parents in the church who had children the same genders and ages as our kids, and over the years we'd vacation together, eat lunch together after church, take turns hosting sleepovers, and have our kids play together. Look for other parents who are raising their children, and find ways to connect with them.

*3. I Will Connect My Kids with Mentors at Church.* Another important benefit of connecting with church families is the opportunity it provides for other adults to influence your kids. Sometimes our children will listen to other adults when they won't listen to us. When these people build relationships with your children, they can reinforce things you are trying to teach. The church is a family, and sometimes our spiritual "aunts and uncles" can make a dramatic difference in a child's life. They can even become their friends.

One of my (Chad) most treasured memories from childhood is a family trip to Disney World with the Sanders family. They don't call it the Magic Kingdom for nothing! It was a magical trip for our family, not just because of the rides but also because we grew in relationship and formed some priceless memories.

The Sanders had been members of our church for almost twenty years, and their son, Jordan, and I were close friends. While I don't recall there being any Bible studies on that trip, I remember playing in the water fountains at Disney World and playing football with Mr. Sanders and Jordan at the hotel. Mr. Sanders eventually became a mentor to me, and at several key moments in my life when I needed wise counsel, I called him on the phone or visited his house. When I needed career advice, was deciding where to go for graduate school, or needed tips on how to negotiate my salary for a job, I had another adult to turn to in addition to my parents, someone outside my family whom I trusted from years of relationship. It was more than just attending church together; we did both church *and* life together.

Our prayer is that God would give you a network of relationships for your kids and that he would give *you* as a gift to other families in your church. In their book *Sticky Faith*, Kara Powell and Chap Clark observe that many youth groups today shoot for a 1:5 ratio of adult sponsors to kids for church activities.[6] A youth group needs about one adult for every five children who attend.

While this is a great principle for a youth group, we love what the authors propose next. Powell and Clark turn the ratio around when it comes to spiritual mentors for youth. They recommend a ratio of 5:1—having five adults pouring into every kid in your church in a variety of ways. These five people could be a combination of a grandparent, a youth minister, an older man or woman from the church, a church member close to the family, and maybe a coach. Powell and Clark advise parents to *ask* other Christians in the church, whoever they may select, to invest in their child. In other words, don't assume this will happen on its own. Pray about it, bring it to the Lord, and ask him to give your children mentors—and give you as a mentor for other children. And then follow up and ask.

Make an effort to know the adults who are ministering to the youth at your church, and take time to build relationships with your children's friends. Not only is this just common sense; it creates accountability with anyone who influences your kids. Many parents underestimate the value of knowing the people in their children's circle of influence. As the Bible says, "Do not be deceived: 'Bad company ruins good morals'" (1 Cor. 15:33 ESV).

Invite the youth leader and his wife to dinner with your family, or host your teenager's small group meeting once a month. Carpool a vanload to the youth group's fall retreat, and you'll have another opportunity to model love for the church and the student ministry. (You might even enjoy yourself!)

# JUST START NOW; DON'T FEEL GUILTY

Yes, it's easier to begin church involvement when your kids are young, but it's never too late to start. As you are building a stronger relationship with your kids, use opportunities in conversation to discuss your new commitment to attending church. Let them see you reading your Bible and signing up for a small group.

Help them develop friends at church by allowing them to attend summer camp or a ski retreat. Gently but firmly insist that they accompany you to weekly services. And, of course, pray.

I (Jason) love being a part of a family of faith. I am thankful to get to hear God's Word taught and value being able to connect with Scripture in a deeper way. I find joy in being encouraged and having an opportunity to encourage others. Church relationships in a fallen world are messy and imperfect, but they are worth it. And the Lord uses them to mature us. When I am struggling personally, I am hungry to be in church to help get my eyes off of my problems and onto the Lord, who is in control.

I try my best to share this love and thankfulness with our kids. I want them to experience the joy of encouragement. I want them to have the opportunity to forgive (and tolerate) imperfect people and learn to be forgiven (and tolerated) by other followers of Jesus. I pray they will find strength in walking with other believers through the valleys in their lives.

I want more for our kids than just going to church on Sunday. I want them to understand that they *are* the church and to know that the church is the gathering of the people of God, not a building. I want them to understand that Jesus demands to be Lord of our lives every day, not just one day a week.

We believe people have time in their lives for the things that are the most important. If you believe this, then it means you will have to make some hard decisions. We urge you to take some time, right now, to think about where the church fits into your life and the life of your family. If it is a high priority for you, then you will likely have many times when you must say no to good things so you can say yes to church. This may mean a lesser commitment to sports or music or dance or a thousand other things. You cannot do it all! You must decide as a family to put God first and to express that by putting a high priority on your active involvement in the local church. We see many families who are way too busy, with far too many commitments—and we see how these commitments become idols that take them away from God's best.

Create a habit of dedication to church involvement in the early years of your children's lives, and set the stage for continued faithfulness. With stakes this high, we simply cannot allow excuses—our children's or ours—to keep us from regular church involvement. Make church a nonnegotiable for your family, beginning now.

## DEDICATION IN ACTION

REMEMBER. Recall God's heart for the church. Memorize Ephesians 3:10 as a family.

> Through the church the manifold wisdom of God [is] made known to the rulers and authorities in the heavenly places. (ESV)

CONSIDER. Think about the specific ways that *your* family contributes to and benefits from your local church. If you have not found a local congregation, what might your family be missing out on that they need right now?

PRAY. Pray how God might be calling your family to engage in the local church.

RESPOND. How is the Holy Spirit leading you *today* to live out your dedication to God in a local church?

LISTEN. "Preeminent" (Col. 1:18), *Purity*, Seeds Family Worship.

# CHAPTER 10

# DEDICATED TO THE KINGDOM OF GOD

IT HAS BEEN OUR DEEP DESIRE to come alongside you as you fully surrender to the Lord's plan for your family. Everything we have been talking about up to this point is connected to something bigger that God is doing. Raising our children to follow Jesus isn't an end in itself; it's part of a greater story, the narrative that drives all of creation. It's the story of the kingdom of God. If we, as parents, learn to fully embrace the kingdom of God in our teaching and in our lives, it will further open a door between heaven and earth for God's power to flow into the world through our families.

The kingdom of God is the central teaching of Jesus.[1] And as disciples and parents who are making disciples of our children, we must pay attention to what Jesus says about the kingdom. He could not stop talking about it, mentioning it more than twenty-five times in the Gospels, and that's just what we have on record.[2] So what exactly *is* the kingdom? And why is it so important in discipling our children?

# THE KINGDOM IS LIKE ...

A kingdom requires a king, and in the kingdom of God, God is the King. As the eternal Son of God, Jesus comes as God in human flesh, the one who rules over God's vast empire. The kingdom of God doesn't refer just to the things we see — the material creation. It's more than a matter of controlling nations and the affairs of state. What is the kingdom of God?

> The kingdom of God is the rule of God over *every* aspect of life, down to the motives and desires of the human heart.

We enter the kingdom of God when we become people who trust and follow Jesus. To much of the world, the kingdom is unknown. But at the end of time, when it is fully consummated, the kingdom of God will be the reality known and experienced in all of creation.

In Jesus Christ, God's kingdom reign is reestablished among us. The kingdom of God is reality, whether we respond to it in obedience, bending our knee to the King, or rebel against it. Yet for people trapped in the power of sin, the kingdom seems distant, like a faint memory of another world. Because the world we live in is fallen and our hearts are inclined to rebel against God's rule, we don't understand what the kingdom is or how it works. We need to learn this, we need to see what the kingdom looks like, and we need to understand how it is entering and transforming our sin-wracked world through the gospel. That's what Jesus came to teach. He came to tell us that the kingdom is accessible here and now through his presence as king and through his work on our behalf.

Jesus spent a great deal of time teaching people about these things. And he helped them to understand the kingdom by using analogies and telling stories. In this way, he engaged his listeners, speaking in a language they could grasp and encouraging them to think for themselves about the work God was doing in the world.[3]

Oftentimes, Jesus would start out by saying, "The kingdom of God is like ..." We suggest that the best way to begin thinking about the kingdom of God and teaching it to your children is to relate it to real life in the same way Jesus did. Jesus told people that the kingdom is like a mustard seed, like leaven that works through dough, and like a treasure hidden in a field (Luke 13:18–19; Matt. 13:33, 44). Through these word pictures, Jesus taught that the kingdom grows in surprising ways (mustard seed and leaven) and that it's worth everything we own (treasure). Using comparisons like these will be the most helpful way to teach your children about the kingdom. Some aspects of the kingdom are indescribable. So let Jesus be your teacher; learn what he says by reading his words, thinking about them, and studying the Gospels to see how he puts his words into action.

## THE KINGDOM AND PARENTING

What does all of this have to do with parenting? As you teach your children to follow Jesus, you'll need to help them understand how their life—and your life together as a family—fits into the bigger purpose of God in the world. Following Jesus isn't just about good parenting or raising children who are morally straight. It's not just about being a good person who avoids evil. It's about joining Jesus in his mission of proclaiming the good news of the kingdom and helping transform the world. This is a new concept for many people, who have been taught a "small" understanding of the gospel.

We just want to encourage parents who did not grow up with an emphasis on God's kingdom to give serious consideration to the kingdom and to its place in the teachings of Jesus. Since it was central to Jesus' teaching, we want to help you make it central to your life and teaching as well.

God confronted me (Jason) with the teaching on the kingdom

CHAD: It wasn't until I was in college that I began to realize the importance of the kingdom of God in Jesus' teaching. And my experience seems to be common. I don't think this was the fault of my parents, as the kingdom of God has been neglected in the recent past. A robust understanding of the kingdom has not typically been emphasized, but this is changing.

Since I left home, my dad and I have had many discussions about this. We both believe that the kingdom of God is essential to the teachings of Jesus, but we're still working out what it means and what it looks like in each of our lives.

when I was leading worship at a family conference in Dallas, Texas, several years ago. Pastor and author David Platt was teaching, and I felt the weight of his message as it landed on the hearts of two thousand church leaders and volunteers who minister to families. His message was simple: God is first and family second. Platt's message forced each of us to stop and take a look at how we had gotten caught up into the flowing stream of our culture by making our families idols. His message, from Luke 14, cut to the heart of what it means to be dedicated to Jesus.

Now great crowds accompanied him, and he turned and said to them, "If anyone comes to me and does not hate his own father and mother and wife and children and brothers and sisters, yes, and even his own life, he cannot be my disciple. Whoever does not bear his own cross and come after me cannot be my disciple. For which of you, desiring to build a tower, does not first sit down and count the cost, whether he has enough to complete it? Otherwise, when he has laid a foundation and is not able to finish, all who see it begin to mock him, saying, 'This man began to build and was not able to finish.' ... So therefore, any one of you who does not renounce all that he has cannot be my disciple."

—Luke 14:25–30, 33 ESV

Platt powerfully shared that the goal of dedicated parents stands in stark contrast to the way our culture wants us to raise our children. He said, "Our goal in parenting is not for our kids ultimately to get a great education, as good as that is; our goal is not for them to be great athletes; our goal is not for them to go on great dates, and find a great husband or great wife; our goal is not for them to have a great career with a great job making great money. *Our goal is for them to love a great God in a way that they will abandon everything this world has to offer in order to follow after him, no matter what he says, no matter what it costs them, and no matter what it costs you.*"[4]

He went on to say that parents need to impart to their children the idea that "God's kingdom is infinitely more important than their family." If this sounds radical to you, know that it's exactly what Jesus taught in Luke 14. Jesus wanted to make it unquestionably clear that following him must take priority over *all* other relationships on earth, including our relationships with our children. To give us a sense of relative priority, he talked about "hating" the people closest to us. It's a strong word that is intended to be unsettling, shaking us out of our comfort zone to wake us up to the idolatry of our hearts.

The truth is that dedicated parents are more dedicated to Jesus than they are to their children. Or perhaps it would be better to say that being dedicated to our children, loving them with the love of God, means that we are dedicated first to Jesus. The same is true of marriage and friendship. To be the best spouse, we must put Jesus first, not our husband or wife. To be the best friend, we must put Jesus first. We love others best when Jesus is the priority in our lives, when we are dedicated to him above all else.

Do we really believe Jesus? Do we believe that if we put other relationships before our call to follow him and love him, we can't be his disciples? We need to ask these hard questions, and we need to let Jesus' words challenge us. Take a moment, pause, and let him do that right now.

Dedicated parents are undeniably more committed to Christ and his kingdom than to anything else on earth, even their own family. The reality of God's reign on earth changes everything for eternity, even the way we see our lives on earth.

## THE KINGDOM IS HERE AND NOW

Jesus made a bold statement: "The kingdom of God is at hand; repent and believe in the gospel" (Mark 1:15 ESV). This was a radical declaration, as radical then as it is today. Jesus was saying that the kingdom is for the *here* and *now*. God's rule, his purposes and plans, his presence in the world, is not something far away or in the distant future. We often think of it as a matter for the *there* and *then*—some place off in the sky after we die. But part of the good news of the kingdom is that we don't have to wait until *then*, because the kingdom is *now*, and it continues forever.[5]

As parents, we easily get caught up in the busyness of the here and now, and we aren't always aware of what God is doing in the here and now. But that's something we need to remember. Ever since Jesus Christ appeared and died for our sins, the long-promised kingdom of God has been present. And now God comes to dwell within us and around us, and to personally rule over us. God's kingdom arrives when we place our faith in Jesus, when we are converted and transferred from one kingdom into another.

## KINGDOMS IN CONFLICT

This conversion happens when we respond to the gospel invitation to put our faith in Jesus. When we trust in him and surrender to him as king instead of trusting in ourselves and making ourselves the rulers of our lives, we are transported from Satan's kingdom into God's kingdom. Colossians 1:13–14 describes the change graphically: "[God] has delivered us from the domain of darkness and transferred us to the kingdom of his beloved Son, in whom we have redemption, the forgiveness of sins" (ESV).

God *is* in control of this world, but in his sovereignty, he allows our spiritual enemy, Satan, to have a limited amount of power. Satan and other evil spirits are real, but Jesus has defeated them, and we are now called to live out that victory in our lives. Each day, we must join the combat, engaging in spiritual warfare. Parents are fighting a very real battle, even if they can't always see their enemy. As we mentioned earlier, the apostle Paul describes this battle in his letter to the Ephesians: "Be strong in the Lord and in the strength of his might. Put on the whole armor of God, that you may be able to stand against the schemes of the devil. For we do not wrestle against flesh and blood, but against the rulers, against the authorities, against the cosmic powers over this present darkness, against the spiritual forces of evil in the heavenly places" (Eph. 6:10 – 12 ESV). Satan has exercised his power throughout history. But now, in Christ, we belong to God's kingdom. We have given our lives into the rightful power of King Jesus.

# THE KINGDOM IN WORD AND DEED

While the expressions of God's power take on many forms, the most helpful way to frame what God's kingdom looks like among his people is that he works through what we say and what we do. Jesus' example shows us how this works. We read that he "went throughout all the cities and villages, teaching in their synagogues and *proclaiming* the gospel of the kingdom and *healing* every disease and every affliction" (Matt. 9:35 ESV, emphasis added). Jesus preached and practiced the kingdom; God used his words and deeds to change the world and the people around him.[6]

The early church lived out the kingdom in this way as well. Paul, for example, preached the gospel in Ephesus for years (the kingdom in word). During that time, he also let God's power work through him (the kingdom in deed): "God was doing extraordinary miracles by the hands of Paul" (Acts 19:11 ESV). This passage shows how God's kingdom works through our words and actions. What a beautiful mystery! These two categories give us a simple framework for understanding how God reigns in this world through his people.

## Word

Jesus told his disciples, "Go into all the world and proclaim the gospel to the whole creation" (Mark 16:15 ESV). Just like Jesus and the early church, we are called to a ministry of sharing God's Word as children of the King. The words we speak can have an amazing impact on people. God uses our simple words to bring the good news about Jesus to their hearts.

I (Chad) have experienced the power of words in living out the Christian life. When I was younger, I enjoyed sharing my faith with others. One way I did this was by calling up my good friends and inviting them to youth group. Many of them came—and kept coming. It was awesome. A few of those friends even stuck around youth group throughout high school, and God changed our lives; he used my invitations as a catalyst to shape our hearts during those years. It all started with *sharing*. I didn't necessarily share a "gospel message," but I opened my mouth to invite others into what God was doing in my life. My friends and I look back on that season as one of the most significant times of spiritual growth for us.

But then, in high school, reality hit, and sharing my faith became harder. Friends changed, and fewer people took their faith as seriously as they did before. While some of my friends followed Jesus, many did not. This is one of the challenges of living in the kingdom: not everyone is open to the invitation. One of my friends in particular represents the challenge of speaking for Christ in the high school years.

We had study hall together, and we talked about God a lot.

My friend presented challenges to Christianity I had never heard before, and sometimes I didn't know how to handle them. Through it all, I learned to engage in spiritual dialogue with my friends at school, bouncing questions off my parents when I needed help. Although this friend and I had many conversations about God, I had never actually shared the gospel with him. So one day I took an opportunity to present it to him after school. I remember being very nervous because he was my friend and because I was really putting myself out there. It was simple: I explained the problem of our sin, the role of the cross, and how Jesus brings us to God.

When I finished, though, it felt like a total bomb. He didn't respond that day, but I know that it was right to share the gospel with him. Perhaps those seeds I planted will bring a harvest for the kingdom one day.

This just goes to show that sharing the Word is like sowing seed (see Mark 4:14–20). Some seed produces fruit, and some does not. We are simply called to be faithful to the gospel, to sow seeds of the Word in the world. This is part of ministry in the kingdom, and it's vital that families nurture a culture of sharing their faith with the world around them. Whatever form your ministry as a family takes, on some level it will involve what you say, so train your kids how to speak for the King.

As important as words are for the kingdom of God, however, it doesn't end with words. We must also live out the reality of the kingdom through our actions.

## Deed

The actions of the kingdom of heaven are sometimes called "justice works," ways of engaging the world for the cause of justice. They can include things like feeding the poor, providing jobs for the unemployed, or visiting prisoners. And though these works of justice come in many forms, they involve action to make things right in the world. These aren't just things we do in church, like volunteering to sing in choir. They are actions we take to communicate to others who God is. Jesus reflected these acts in his healing ministry. He performed miracles and restored people to physical health through his *divinity*. God does not always give us miraculous ministries, but we can learn from the life of Jesus that God cares about people's physical needs. In addition to sharing the gospel, we can minister to the needs people have. Part of Jesus' ministry involved making the physical world around him right, giving people a glimpse of what life under God's rule looks like. We seek to do the same through the work of the Holy Spirit.

All of this might sound great, but you are probably wondering, How do I do any of this? Where do I get started? One practical way to begin engaging the world like this as a family is based on the "Before-During-After" model outlined in the book *Sticky Faith*. Think about an activity you can engage in together as a family. Look around for needs in your neighborhood, or talk with your pastor about ways to serve the community. Start your activity by framing the experience *beforehand*, help your kids process the experience *during the event*, and have a debriefing *afterward*.[7] This gives your family an opportunity to serve and to learn about serving through action. By talking with your children about what you do together, you gain a better understanding of how they are thinking. You can use these times to train them in how to love a lost and hurting world so they can become lifelong disciples in the kingdom of God. You are also showing them that holistic kingdom work involves the whole person. We tell others about Jesus, but we also need to show them Jesus by what we do.

An important lesson for parents to teach their children is that we're serving people, not accomplishing projects. We will be the first to admit that we have not done this perfectly, often focusing on projects instead of people, but we've put ourselves out there and tried to learn from our failures.[8] These types of struggles can also be teachable moments for the family.

If you aren't comfortable with engaging in service activities alone, join up with others in your church and serve together. To get you started, here are a few examples of what serving others for the sake of God's kingdom can look like:

## Jason

Our family has been involved in serving people from the other side of the world without ever leaving our town of Twin Falls, Idaho. There are an astonishing number of refugees who live in our town because of a program run by the College of Southern Idaho. Every year, with the help of the college, our church reaches out to these refugee families during the holidays by providing them with meals on both Thanksgiving and Christmas. The church donates food and money, and then families pack and deliver the meals. The weekend before Christmas this past year, we packed a school bus with food boxes and church family members and headed out to demonstrate the love of Christ. Some of the families we met had recently arrived in America from the Sudan, Bhutan, and Iran, to name just a few countries. Though many of the people didn't speak English, I brought my guitar and we sang "O Come Let Us Adore Him" and "Joy to the World" and invited them to come fellowship with us whenever possible. The generosity of Christ through our church, accompanied by the joy in our songs, bridged the gap between our worlds.

## Bobby

When my children were young, for a period of time we set aside one Saturday a month for Meals on Wheels, a local charity that connects Christians with the poor to provide them a hot meal. We took our kids to the H. G. Hills grocery store to pick up the hot food in takeout boxes. They stood in line with us as we purchased food and drinks. Then, after we arrived at the apartment complex, we hand-delivered each meal to the people on our list. They were beautiful people, but very different from us. What a joy it was to serve them! They treated us with kindness and gratitude. We encouraged Ashley and Chad to knock on the doors, greet people, and talk with them as we gave them the food boxes. The whole experience—from picking up the food to talking with the strangers—gave the kids an opportunity to show the love of God with their hands and feet.

## Chad

When I was in high school, my family and I went on a mission trip to Mexico to work with a local church. At the time, it seemed like an overwhelming experience, because it was one of my first trips out of the English-speaking world. Looking back, though, I'm grateful that my parents exposed me to other cultures. Sometimes it's hard to tell what God is up to in the moment, but I have to think, deep in the recesses of my heart, that God was cultivating in me a love for people who are different from me.

Years later, in my midtwenties, I found myself gravitating to serving the poor and seeking justice in my city. God led me and a few friends as we moved into a low-income apartment complex, where we met refugees from Iraq, Burundi, Sudan, DR Congo, and Burma. Over the next few years, I was able to develop relationships with these new friends as I continued to learn about God's kingdom among the materially poor.

When I was young, my parents and my church created opportunities for me to be comfortable around different kinds of people, and as I got older, I started taking initiative on my own, not because I had to but because I had a vision for what the kingdom of God looks like in the here-and-now events of daily life. I'm so grateful that my parents passed on to me God's heart for using my hands, feet, and voice for the kingdom.

◆　◆　◆

What we describe is just a sample of what it means to participate in the kingdom of God. Remember, we do it through word and deed. Both are vital. As your family embraces this understanding of discipleship, consider how together you can impact the world for the gospel.

## CONCLUSION

The biggest shift we've experienced in thinking about and reflecting on the kingdom of God is a change in our vision. Understanding the kingdom of God has helped us to see that this isn't just about our families or our local church. It's bigger than that. This is global. It's cosmic. It begins with the eternal God creating this world out of nothing and continues to this day, from generation to generation and far into the future. When you surrender your life to God, you join something far bigger than your family, even beyond your church or denomination. God's everlasting kingdom begins now and continues forever.

We look forward to a rich welcome with you when God's kingdom comes in all its fullness. Now we experience it only in part, but one day we'll experience his eternal kingdom with every struggle ended, every enemy defeated, and every tear wiped clean. May that day come soon!

## DEDICATION IN ACTION

REMEMBER. The kingdom is accessible for believers *here* and *now*, not just after we die. Memorize Colossians 1:13–14 as a family.

> [God] has delivered us from the domain of darkness and transferred us to the kingdom of his beloved Son, in whom we have redemption, the forgiveness of sins. (ESV)

CONSIDER. Jesus spoke about the kingdom more than twenty-five times. He said it is like a mustard seed, like leaven, and like a treasure in a field (Luke 13:18–19; Matt. 13:33, 44). How do you understand Jesus' teaching about the kingdom of God?

PRAY. Ask God to help you understand his kingdom and live faithfully in it here and now.

RESPOND. How is the Holy Spirit leading you *today* to live out your dedication to the kingdom of God?

LISTEN. "Seek First" (Matt. 6:31–34), *Seeds of Purpose*, Seeds Family Worship.

# DEDICATED TODAY

## TODAY'S CHALLENGES

As we've said throughout this book, there are many challenges and additional complexities for parents today. After years of pastoral ministry and personal experience, we know one thing for sure: discipling your children needs to be your top priority.

We want our children to be happy. And yes, we want our children to get good grades. Yes, we want our children to be good at sports. Yes, we want our children to be talented dancers, musicians, and many other things. But there is nothing more important than training our children to trust and follow Jesus and obey all of his teachings. Our children were created to glorify God and enjoy him forever. And in the end, when all is said and done, that's what matters.

As parents, we must do our part in helping them become the people God created them to be. We cannot delegate the discipleship of our children to the church, to youth pastors, or to Christian schools. God has given the responsibility to us (Deut. 6:6–9; Eph. 6:4). His primary plan for discipleship is parents teaching their children by the power of the Holy Spirit.

# DEDICATED

Over the past twenty years, I (Bobby) have seen many high school graduations. Two churches I have been a part of set aside time at the end of the school year to celebrate high school graduates by hosting a special, personalized ceremony and banquet. At this ceremony, the parents and the seniors speak. For many of these seniors, the trajectory of their young life has been set. There are some who have been discipled, and they often stand out from their peers. They are young men and women with strong convictions, a faith that has been strengthened through persecution in their high school years, and a clear sense of direction. They stand out because they know who they are and whose they are. My hope and prayer is that every graduate in our church would be one of those students.

And yet, one of the greatest temptations parents face is to build a kingdom of family instead of introducing children to the kingdom of God. While a renewed focus on family in our broken society is wonderful, there is a risk that in our zeal to recover the family, we will build a *self-centered* kingdom, one that is about our ambition, our dreams, our pride, one that ultimately points people to look at us and what we have accomplished. In many ways, this is the self-same, corrupted American dream. It whispers a false advertisement to us: *Seek a successful career first, build a great reputation for yourself, and focus on financial security.* For parents, the message becomes, *Give your children the best opportunities to succeed, get them into the best school, and help them find the best career.* These are not bad things necessarily, but they are typically self-focused, not God-focused.

You can raise nice kids who will look successful and appear capable, but they may not be working for the kingdom of God. We can promote values that look good on the outside—like hard work and self-reliance—but these same values can easily lead our children to focus on the kingdom of self, not on the kingdom of God. It's easy to do this. The messages are all over billboards, com-

174

mercials, and social media. But if we take the teaching of Jesus to heart, we will seek first God's kingdom, not these other things, trusting our heavenly Father to provide (Matt. 6:31–34). God will always provide what we need, but he will not always give us what we want.

Sometimes the path God uses to teach our children is not the path we would choose for them. He may use circumstances and situations that break our hearts and cause anguish in our families. God never promises us that this will be easy. But remember, the goal isn't to have nice, successful kids. It's to have kids who love Jesus, trust him, and will follow him at the cost of everything else.

In Jesus' longest and most well-known sermon, he warned his disciples to be on guard against the kingdom of self: "No one can serve two masters, for either he will hate the one and love the other, or he will be devoted to the one and despise the other. You cannot serve God and money" (Matt. 6:24 ESV). We are created for God's kingdom, and every other kingdom we attempt to build will one day be destroyed, perhaps sooner than we expect.

For parents living in the United States—one of the wealthiest nations in the history of the world—your everyday choices will impact your children. They're learning basic principles of kingdom building all the time just by watching you. You have great influence over your children! So are you allowing God full control of your life?

What kingdom are you preparing your children for? The typical pattern of our culture is to raise children who go to college, make money, and pursue the dreams of this world. Families go to great lengths to sacrifice, save, and make this dream a reality. And as important as it is to seek an education for our children and to want the very best for them, above all else we want God's kingdom vision to guide them as they leave the home. That can mean going to college after high school, or it might mean not going.

There is no single right path for every child. Instead we must seek God with our children to see what the Lord has for them. Many young people go to college and struggle with their faith. Some walk away from the church. Some return. Some choose not to go to college, and experience the same choices. What matters is that you pray for your children and seek God's best with them, instead of falling in line with what the world defines as successful.

# BE TRANSFORMED

If we are going to be dedicated parents who parent based on what the Bible teaches rather than what the culture says is good and right, then we need our families to look different from those in the world. The apostle Paul tells us in Romans 12 that our entire life is an act of worship, a response to God's mercies. As you are seeking the transformation of God in your life, remember that it starts with his mercies, which enable us to surrender to him. Our job isn't just to

CHAD: My high school years were a battle for my faith. But now, looking back, I understand that God was making my faith stronger. What felt overwhelming as a teenager is now a good thing for my faith as an adult. I often felt alone in high school, even though I had good friends. But following Christ is not always popular, even in religious circles. Truly being a disciple will create times of difficulty, loneliness, and rejection— even times of being hated by others. I got a little taste of that truth in high school.

When those same challenges come today, I see them as part of being a disciple. Paul told Timothy, his young disciple, "*All* who desire to live a godly life in Christ Jesus will be persecuted" (2 Tim. 3:12 ESV, emphasis added). I've learned how personal and real the love of God is through the difficulties, and that alone has been worth it.

try hard. It's to turn to God, one day at a time, asking for his help as we take positive steps toward discipling our children. "Do not conform to the pattern of this world, but be transformed by the renewing of your mind. Then you will be able to test and approve what God's will is—his good, pleasing and perfect will" (Rom. 12:2).

In writing this letter, Paul was addressing the Christians in Rome, who were facing their own struggles to fully surrender to God. We believe that this same principle of transformation applies to parenting as well. There may be some of you reading this book who are feeling discouraged right now. If you feel you're not living up to what God has called you to as a parent, we want you to know there's hope. God can transform your life. Both parents and kids are dealing with cultural pressures, and God will use these to mature your whole family as you walk through them together.

# DON'T JUST GO THROUGH THE MOTIONS

We want to encourage you to commit to making whatever changes are necessary to live out your dedication as parents. The following song was written by Jason Houser, Matthew West, and Sam Mizell about living your life fully for God, but we think it applies just as well to our call to be dedicated parents.

### THE MOTIONS
This might hurt, it's not safe
But I know that I've gotta make a change
I don't care if I break
At least I'll be feeling something

'Cause just okay is not enough
Help me fight through the nothingness of life

I don't wanna go through the motions
I don't wanna go one more day
Without Your all-consuming passion inside of me

I don't wanna spend my whole life asking
What if I had given everything
Instead of going through the motions?

No regrets, not this time
I'm gonna let my heart defeat my mind
Let Your love make me whole
I think I'm finally feeling something

'Cause just okay is not enough
Help me fight through the nothingness of this life

'Cause I don't wanna go through the motions
I don't wanna go one more day
Without Your all-consuming passion inside of me

I don't wanna spend my whole life asking
What if I had given everything
Instead of going through the motions?

Take me all the way

I don't wanna go through the motions
I don't wanna go one more day
Without Your all-consuming passion inside of me

I don't wanna spend my whole life asking
What if I had given everything
Instead of going through the motions?

# THE DEDICATED CHALLENGE

Regardless of your stage in parenting, you have a challenging but joyful road ahead of you. As we close, we want to summarize the vision we have put before you, in the form of a challenge. We hope you will respond like Joshua, an example of a dedicated parent from the Old Testament. He faced a decision when he was leading the people of God at a critical point of history. Many people were tempted to leave the way and pursue idols and other gods.

This temptation is similar to enticements that lure parents today to pursue other kingdoms and worldly success for their family. In the midst of this struggle, Joshua stood up and issued a challenge to the people, one that speaks to Christian parents today: "Choose this day whom you will serve.... As for me and my house, we will serve the LORD" (Josh. 24:15 ESV). That's the heart of the Dedicated Challenge. It means stepping up and saying, "As for me and my house, we will serve the Lord, by *making discipleship our top family priority.*"

We have given you many ideas to consider as your family seeks God. What we offer now are the essential elements of dedicated parenting, the nuts and bolts of our message. These are practical takeaways for you to remember as you train your children in the ways of Jesus in our culture today. You might want to print this out and post it somewhere as a reminder of what God is calling you to as a parent.

Our definition of discipleship for parents assumes daily intentionality. The core challenge to be dedicated to discipleship is the over arching principle that encompasses every aspect of spiritual parenting:

Train your children to trust and follow Jesus.

This challenge is focused on making five commitments.

1. Pursue Jesus first and foremost. "I am the vine; you are the branches. Whoever abides in me and I in him, he it is that bears much fruit, for apart from me you can do nothing" (John 15:5 ESV).
2. Love your children by spending time with them. "A new commandment I give to you, that you love one another: just as I have loved you, you also are to love one another. By this all people will know that you are my disciples, if you have love for one another" (John 13:34–35 ESV).

3. Teach your children obedience to Jesus daily. "Go and make disciples of all nations, baptizing them in the name of the Father and of the Son and of the Holy Spirit, and teaching them to obey everything I have commanded you. And surely I am with you always, to the very end of the age" (Matt. 28:19–20).

4. Lead your family in worship regularly. "Hear, O Israel: The LORD our God, the LORD is one. You shall love the LORD your God with all your heart and with all your soul and with all your might. And these words that I command you today shall be on your heart. You shall teach them diligently to your children, and shall talk of them when you sit in your house, and when you walk by the way, and when you lie down, and when you rise" (Deut. 6:4–7 ESV).

5. *Seek expressions of God's kingdom through word and deed with your family.* "Jesus went throughout all the cities and villages, teaching in their synagogues and proclaiming the gospel of the kingdom and healing every disease and every affliction" (Matt. 9:35 ESV).

Taking the Dedicated Challenge is simply saying yes to these commitments. *Yes, I will be dedicated in these areas by the power of the Holy Spirit to the glory of God.*

Will you step up and take the Dedicated Challenge?

Just as Jesus encourages the Christians in the book of Revelation to be faithful and courageous in a time of tremendous spiritual conflict and war, we challenge you to lead your family to be faithful, courageous followers of Christ (Rev. 13:7). One day soon we will be sending our children out into the world, and they will continue fighting the spiritual war out there. Knowing this affects how we train and prepare them. Their eternal destiny may lie in the balance, and we want to leave them well prepared for that day when they are out on their own. The stakes cannot be higher.

It starts now. Stepping up is costly, yes, but you will reap what you sow. Sow for eternal life. Teach your children to be disciples of Christ Jesus so that one day you will join with them and together, at the end of history, receive from God the victor's crown. Focus on that day. Prepare now. We invite you to pray this prayer as your commitment to the Dedicated Challenge:

*Father, in every challenge I face, may I run to you. Heal me of spiritual blindness that is keeping me from seeing the truth and from making discipleship of my children my top priority as a parent.*

*Your Word says to set my mind on things above, not on the things on earth, because I have died and my life is hidden with Christ. Give me the courage to die to self and to set my mind on you and your kingdom. I pray that you will give me vision and commitment that reaches past the here and now, and give me a glimpse of my family in light of eternity.*

*Lord, this challenge is bigger than me and my abilities, but you promised to be with me, and I believe that your promises are true. You began a good work in me, and you are going to finish it. So, Lord, I cry out to you to be my help, my refuge, and my shield as I seek to walk out this great calling.*

*In Jesus' name, amen.*

# DEDICATED
# TO MARRIAGE

ONE OF THE KEY PARTS of being a dedicated parent is having a healthy marriage. In this appendix, we want to offer some suggestions as you strive for a marriage that is vibrant and Christ-centered. If you are married, it is essential that you put a loving relationship with your spouse above your relationship with your children. That means God first, the marriage second, and the children third.

The dynamics of the marriage relationship—the way that husband and wife interact with one another—sets the tone for how relationships in the home work. The foundation of the home is the unity created by God, who teaches that in marriage "the two will become one" (Matt. 19:5). Parents must be committed to unity with each other. Like Jesus said, "If a house is divided against itself, that house will not be able to stand" (Mark 3:25 ESV). Your unity as a couple will give amazing stability to your home.

The reality for many of us, though, is that we come from homes with broken marriages. Maybe your parents didn't know God's purpose for marriage, let alone try to build a home around it. Or maybe your marriage is currently being attacked. The enemy tries to destroy marriages, because he knows how important family relationships are for spiritual health. God designed the family to be the place where we learn what it means to trust and follow Jesus.

What happens when a marriage is unhealthy? As time goes on, the honeymoon phase of marriage passes, and reality hits. You see the other person's flaws and bad habits that you didn't see before, and the commitment becomes challenging. This is a perfect place for God's redemption, because one of the purposes of marriage is to form us to be more like Jesus.

# THE GOOD NEWS ABOUT BUILDING A CHRIST-CENTERED MARRIAGE

Christian marriage is often illustrated using a triangle with God at the top and each spouse at the bottom, on opposite corners. The closer each individual gets to the Lord, the closer they will be to one another. This is because marriage is a sacred commitment made first with the Lord, and then with your spouse.

God designed marriage to be an illustration of the "profound mystery" (Eph. 5:32) of Christ's relationship with the church. The apostle Paul says that when two people become one flesh in marriage, "it refers to Christ and the church" (Eph. 5:32 ESV). Timothy Keller, in his book *The Meaning of Marriage* (which we highly recommend), describes the mystery of marriage by saying, "Marriage, next to our relationship with God, is the most profound relationship that there is. And that is why, like knowing God himself, coming to know and love your spouse is difficult and painful yet rewarding and wondrous."[1] The purpose of marriage is to reveal the deep mystery of Christ's love for the church, and living within God's purpose for marriage is the first step of building a home dedicated to discipleship.

Shanti Feldhahn is a marriage expert who has written on the relationships between men and women, especially in marriage.

She is the author of two bestselling books, *For Women Only* and *For Men Only*. Her most recent books on marriage summarize some of the latest research on how marriages endure and what makes people happy in marriage.[2] *The Good News about Marriage* shows us that the state of marriage in the USA is more positive than commonly thought. And in the book *The Surprising Secrets of Highly Happy Marriages*, Feldhahn asked roughly one thousand couples to identify their level of happiness in marriage (self-defined). Her research demonstrates some important and encouraging patterns. Here are five principles for building a good marriage that we developed based on the findings in her research.

1. *Be encouraged.* The real divorce rate is less than 30 percent, which is much lower than commonly thought, and it shows us that many more people work to keep their marriage commitments than previously thought.[3]
2. *Hang on.* The majority of people who are unhappily married (and considering divorce) but stay together report that they are happily married five years later.[4]
3. *Engage in church community.* The divorce rate of people who regularly attend church is 25 – 50 percentage points lower compared with that of people who do not regularly attend church.[5]
4. *Pursue God.* We pursue God for God's glory alone, but as a side result, people with an active Christian faith are statistically among the happiest in marriage.[6] Even if this were not the case, peace with God enables many people to handle ongoing difficulties.
5. *Remember the little things.* Most marriage problems can be fixed by small changes.[7]

This research is good news. To couples who are in the midst of difficulties, it's not too late. You can still build your marriage from what you have.[8] It's never too late for God's redemption, if you're willing. And to young couples, focus on building your marriage before you get to the point where you are desperate for help.

# WHEN THE LORD BUILDS A HOME

In order to lead family worship in your home, it is critical to allow God to build your marriage on the foundation of Christ. The psalmist writes, "Unless the LORD builds the house, the builders labor in vain" (Ps. 127:1). This verse means that God is the architect and builder of strong homes. When we try to build a home apart from him, it doesn't amount to anything of substance. It's vanity. Since marriage frames the home, it's important to get this relationship right. If you don't build your marriage, with God's help, on who Jesus is and who he taught us to be, you are building your home on sand. When the storms come (and they will come), your house will fall with a great crash (Matt. 7:24–27). That is why the foundation of a solid home is trusting and following Christ, and a house built on Christ is a safe haven in which children come to know the Lord.

The ultimate purpose of marriage is much greater than to feel happy or to find fulfillment; it's to reveal God. When your children see you and your spouse loving each other with humility, service, and sacrifice, they will see God in your relationship, because it's only by God's grace that you can live this way. With Christ, spiritual parents can build a solid family legacy. Christ creates an atmosphere of love and support as children grow up, make choices, and ask questions.

# DEDICATED AS A SINGLE PARENT

**WHEN HER HUSBAND STOPPED BREATHING,** Lyneve went from wife to widow within a few hours. Though doctors tried to save her husband, he died in the hospital after a sudden heart attack. Losing Tim was the hardest thing she had ever been through, but following the funeral, she found she was now overwhelmed with the pressures of grieving with her two boys and learning how to survive without her husband.

In a single day, Lyneve became a single parent. Her struggles after her husband's death are common for many single parents. The responsibilities can be overwhelming when you are by yourself. Perhaps you're a mom who needs to find a second job to make ends meet financially. You still have to take care of a household, and you don't have enough hands to do everything that needs to be done — cleaning the house, making dinner, taking out the trash. The list goes on and on. On top of that, you have the personal and emotional challenges of being single again. You're simply trying to survive as a single parent. You read this book and wonder, *How is this possible for me?*

You're not alone. God makes it possible, because he will partner with you. He will help you in personal ways. Like the psalmist
says,

> Cast your burden on the LORD,
>     and he will sustain you;
> he will never permit
>     the righteous to be moved.
>
> —*Psalm 55:22 ESV*

This psalm was written to console a person who had been
hurt by someone close to them. Consolation is what you need
when you experience the death of a spouse, or abandonment or
divorce—someone *very* close is now out of your life. In the middle of the pain, remember that God is involved in your everyday
life. He knows your situation, and he loves you. That's why you
can be confident in bringing your burdens to the Lord.

Look to the church as an extension of God's love for you. Paul
warns us against pride in the body of Christ when he talks about
how we each offer unique spiritual gifts: "The eye cannot say to
the hand, 'I have no need of you'" (1 Cor. 12:21 ESV). Similarly,
we cannot say to other people in the church, "I don't need you."
So as a single parent, prayerfully discern whom within the church
to invite into your family to help raise your kids. That means,
first, that you must be connected and committed to a local church
(which we address in chapter 9, "Dedicated to Church"), but also
that you rely on the Lord in boldness to do a difficult thing: ask
another couple or individual in the church to help disciple your
children. This calls for wisdom, so ask the Lord for personal direction. While it's ideal to connect with people from your church,
sometimes God brings other positive Christian influences into
your family's life from outside your church.

Your challenge as a single parent is different from the challenge
that married couples face in raising kids. Children naturally per-

ceive single parents differently. They rely on you because you're the only parent they have (or the only parent they really know).

Here are five key principles that we recommend for single parents who desire to make discipleship the top priority in their home.

1. Stay connected with the Lord. Pray and read the Bible every day. It is important to "abide" in your relationship with Christ. Jesus said, "I am the vine; you are the branches. Whoever abides in me and I in him, he it is that bears much fruit, for apart from me you can do nothing" (John 15:5 ESV). For single parents, this means that you will find your strength from your true self in Christ, by spending regular time with him. Through reading the Bible, you can listen to what he has to say to you, and through prayer, you can stay connected with him.

2. Stay connected to your church. We mentioned earlier that your kids need the church, and now we want to emphasize your relationship with the body of Christ. You personally, as an adult, need the church. You need the friendship, support, and prayer of others.

3. Seek out a parenting mentor. It is common for people who need outside support in difficult situations in life to have a mentor or a sponsor. Single parents will greatly benefit from personal biblical counsel from another Christian parent. Your perspective can easily become clouded by isolation. So ask the Lord to help you find a person who will help you perceive blind spots in your spiritual walk and in your parenting, and who will also encourage you and celebrate victories with you.

4. Be authentic about your struggles as a family. Your children will likely grieve because of their broken

family, and it's important that you do not hide your pain. By showing your grief, you help your children process their pain as well. They see that it hurts you, and you can show them how to deal with heartache and difficulties in a healthy way. In fact, as strange as it may sound, it's important to teach your children how to grieve. You have the opportunity to share your struggle and teach them what to do with their emotions.

5. Receive God's grace. Be gentle with yourself. Receiving God's grace means learning to forgive yourself and let go of your past mistakes. God does not expect flawless perfection, and he knows that mistakes and brokenness are part of our lives. Allow his grace to extend into your heart as you become more like him. His love will restore you.

# A SUCCESS STORY

Wanda Pratt had her first child at age eighteen. She had another child three years later. By the time she was twenty, she was a single parent raising two boys. They moved from apartment to apartment, but she refused to lose hope that they would make it. She made sure to attend her younger son's basketball games when she could, and in the summer she would even make him wake up in the middle of the night to run hills and do push-ups. Against all odds, her son made it into the NBA, and when he became the 2014 MVP, he attributed his success to his mother. This player is Kevin Durant.

In his moving award speech, Kevin thanked various people in his life for helping him get there, but he gave the ultimate thanks to his mom, who raised him and his brother on her own. "We wasn't supposed to be here. You made us believe. You kept us off the street. You put clothes on our backs, food on the table. When you didn't eat, you made sure we ate. You went to sleep hungry. You sacrificed for us." Then he gave his mom the highest compliment he could in that moment: "You the real MVP."

Our point in telling this story is not to highlight Kevin Durant's success from the world's point of view but to point out how God can use single parents to raise children who trust and follow Jesus through difficult circumstances. Wanda Pratt took the narrow road of single parenting by instilling her faith in her boys. She made it a priority to be involved in the church, and now Durant has a spiritual coach and goes to chapel before games. This shows the fruit of her commitment in Kevin Durant's life today. She could have easily given in to the culture, but she raised her boys to know the Lord. Both Wanda Pratt and Kevin Durant give God the credit for his success.

# NOTES

## Chapter 1: Dedicated to Discipleship

1. Dallas Willard, *The Great Omission: Reclaiming Jesus's Essential Teachings on Discipleship* (San Francisco: HarperSanFrancisco, 2006), xi.

2. These leaders include Bill Hull, Jeff Vanderstelt, Jim Putman, Francis Chan, K. P. Yohannan, Robert Coleman, Dann Spader, Pat Morley, Kennon Vaughn, Robbie Gallaty, and Alan Hirsch. Bobby Harrington is the founder of Discipleship.org. See Bobby Harrington and Josh Patrick, *Discipleship Handbook* (Discipleship.org, 2013) and Jim Putman and Bobby Harrington with Robert Coleman, *DiscipleShift: Five Steps That Help Your Church Make Disciples Who Make Disciples* (Grand Rapids, Mich.: Zondervan, 2013).

3. Christian Smith, *Soul Searching: The Religious and Spiritual Lives of American Teenagers* (New York: Oxford University Press, 2005), 54.

4. Merton P. Strommen and Irene A. Strommen, *Five Cries of Parents* (Minneapolis: Youth and Family Institute, 1993), 134.

5. George Barna, *Transforming Children into Spiritual Champions* (Ventura, Calif.: Gospel Light, 2003), 78.

6. Ibid., 56.

7. Joe White, *Faith Training* (Colorado Springs: Focus on the Family, 1994), 97.

8. Ibid., 98.

## Chapter 2: Dedicated to Relationships

1. Cited by Thomas L. Friedman in "Foreign Affairs; Cyber-Serfdom," *New York Times* (January 30, 2001), *www.nytimes.com/2001/01/30/opinion/foreign-affairs-cyber-serfdom.html.*

2. For more on grace-filled parenting, see Jeff VanVonderan, *Families Where Grace Is in Place* (Grand Rapids, Mich.: Bethany House, 1992).

3. George Barna, *Revolutionary Parenting: What the Research Shows Really Works* (Carol Stream, Ill.: BarnaBooks, 2007), 33.

4. Joe White, *Faith Training* (Colorado Springs: Focus on the Family, 1994), 17, emphasis added.

5. Gary D. Chapman, *The Five Love Languages of Children* (Chicago: Northfield, 2012).

## Chapter 3: Dedicated to Spiritual Parenting

1. David Kinnaman, *You Lost Me: Why Young Christians Are Leaving Church ... and Rethinking Faith* (Grand Rapids, Mich.: Baker, 2011), 22.

2. Scot McKnight, *The Jesus Creed* (Brewster, Mass.: Paraclete Press, 2004), 7, 298.

3. "*Shanan*," HALOT, 4:1607.

4. The concept of "cheating" things in your life can be confusing. We highly recommend reading *Choosing to Cheat* (Colorado Springs: Multnomah, 2003) if you are hungry for more on this framework. Andy Stanley mentions this concept throughout the book.

## Chapter 4: Dedicated to Jesus

1. The basic framework of this chapter was first presented in Bill Hull and Bobby Harrington in the book *Evangelism or Discipleship: Can They Effectively Work Together?* (Centerville, Va.: Exponential, 2014).

2. John A. Phillips, *The Form of Christ in the World: A Study of Bonhoeffer's Christology* (London: Collins, 1967), 100.

3. We commend the broad outline of Scot McKnight's, *The King Jesus Gospel: The Original Good News Revisited* (Grand Rapids, Mich.: Zondervan, 2011).

4. Robert Picirilli does a great job of showing how the emphasis that we are saved "by grace through faith" and discipleship coalesce. *Discipleship: The Expression of Saving Faith* (Nashville: Randall House, 2013).

# NOTES

5. Some traditions describe the physical expression differently than we do. They might say, "Engage the sacraments of baptism and confirmation as concrete and covenant expressions of faith."

## Chapter 5: Dedicated to Family Worship

1. See the end of this chapter for a list of recommended resources.
2. Voddie Bauckham, *Family Driven Faith* (Wheaton, Ill.: Crossway, 2007), 139–42.
3. Quoted in Bob Rienow, *Visionary Parenting* (Nashville: Randall House, 2009), 98.

## Chapter 6: Dedicated to the Word

1. *http://en.wikipedia.org/wiki/International_Bureau_of_Weights_and_Measures* (February 3, 2014).
2. John Willis, *God and Man: Then and Now* (Austin, Tex.: Sweet Publishing, 1974), 55.
3. Eric Geiger, Michael Kelley, and Philip Nation, *Transformational Discipleship: How People Really Grow* (Nashville: B&H Publishing, 2012), Kindle ed., 910–18.
4. Greg L. Hawkins and Cally Parkinson, Move: *What 1,000 Churches Reveal about Spiritual Growth* (Grand Rapids, Mich.: Zondervan, 2011), 10.
5. Dwight L. Moody, *Leadership*, vol. 10, no. 4 (Fall 1989).
6. Quoted in Michael Green, *Illustrations for Biblical Preaching* (Grand Rapids, Mich.: Baker, 1989), 35.

## Chapter 7: Dedicated to Prayer

1. See Richard Bauckham's chapter on sanctification as dedication in the gospel of John, "The Holiness of Jesus and His Disciples in the Gospel of John," in *The Testimony of the Beloved Disciple* (Grand Rapids, Mich.: Baker Academic, 2007), 253–70.
2. Mark Holman, *Faith Begins at Home* (Ventura, Calif.: Regal, 2005), 87.

## Chapter 8: Dedicated to Discipline

1. Chip Ingram, *Effective Parenting in a Defective World* (Colorado Springs: Focus on the Family, 2007).
2. John MacAuthor, *Hebrews*, MacAuthor Bible Studies (Chicago: Moody, 1983), 395.

## Chapter 9: Dedicated to the Church

1. Aristotle, *Politics*, book 1, section II.
2. For more information, see Joshua Harris's popular book *Stop Dating the Church: Fall in Love with the Family of God* (Sisters, Ore.: Multnomah, 2004).
3. Harris, *Stop Dating the Church*, 21–22.
4. David Kinnaman, *You Lost Me: Why Young Christians Are Leaving Church ... And Rethinking Faith* (Grand Rapids: Baker Books, 2011), 25.
5. Ibid., 27.
6. Kara E. Powell and Chap Clark, *Sticky Faith: Everyday Ideas to Build Lasting Faith in Your Kids* (Grand Rapids, Mich.: Zondervan, 2011), 101.

## Chapter 10: Dedicated to the Kingdom of God

1. One of the most helpful books on this topic, summing up the recent scholarly dialogue and pointing to a solid integration of the teaching in the church, is Scot McKnight, *Kingdom Conspiracy: Returning to the Radical Mission of the Local Church* (Grand Rapids, Mich.: Brazos, 2014).
2. Here are the unique occurrences of "kingdom of God" in the English Standard Version: Matt. 4:17//Mark 1:15; Matt. 5:3//Luke 6:20; Matt. 5:19–20//Luke 16:16; Matt. 6:33//Luke 12:31; Matt. 8:11–12//Luke 13:28–29; Matt. 12:22//Luke 11:20; Matt. 12:28//Mark 3:24; Matt. 13:31//Mark 4:30//Luke 13:18; Matt. 13:33//Luke 13:20; Matt. 13:11//Mark 4:11//Luke 8:10; Matt. 16:28//Mark 9:1//Luke 9:27; Matt. 18:3//Mark 10:15//Luke 18–17; Matt. 19:14//Mark 10:14//Luke 18:16; Matt. 19:24–25//Mark 10:23–25//Luke 18:24–25; Matt. 21:13//Luke 7:28; Matt. 21:43; Matt. 26:29//Mark 14:25//Luke 22:16–18; Mark 4:26; 9:27; 12:34; Luke 4:43; 9:60, 62; 10:9, 11; 17:20; 18:28; 21:31; John 3:3, 5. Many of the parallels are "kingdom of heaven" instead of "kingdom of God," but the meaning is similar.

   See also "kingdom of heaven," although most occurrences of this phrase are in Matthew. Matthew's phrase often overlaps with Mark and Luke's "kingdom of God," so the above list is almost exhaustive of both "kingdom of God" and "kingdom of heaven."
3. For further reading on the kingdom of God, see N. T. Wright, *The Challenge of Jesus: Rediscovering Who Jesus Was and Is* (Downers Grove, Ill.: InterVarsity, 1999).

# NOTES

4. David Platt, D-6 Conference in Dallas, Texas, 2012.
5. The kingdom is fully realized later, but it starts now. See Mark 14:25 for the kingdom fully consummated. See also Acts 1:3–7.
6. This is a simplified way to think of the kingdom that merely introduces the means of God's work among his people. Two important notes: (1) Jesus' miracles of healing affirm the importance of our actions, but these are not equal. They are similar in terms of value: Christ's miracles affirm the importance of a person's body, and so do our actions. That's all we are saying. (2) God's kingdom is not necessarily limited to coming through people's words and deeds. He has the capacity to work through any means he decides.
7. Kara E. Powell and Chap Clark, *Sticky Faith: Everyday Ideas to Build Lasting Faith in Your Kids* (Grand Rapids, Mich.: Zondervan, 2011), 137–39.
8. Corbett and Fikkert address this in *When Helping Hurts: How to Alleviate Poverty without Hurting the Poor—and Yourself* (Chicago: Moody, 2009), 81. They offer a Christian perspective on poverty. They approach the issue from a holistic perspective, so that when we interact with the poor, we see them as a whole person. The work of God's kingdom, they say, is *relational*, so when Adam and Eve sinned in the Garden of Eden, their relationships were broken. This is what defines poverty in general. We all need recovery from a broken relationship with God, with self, with other people, and with creation: "Poverty alleviation is the ministry of reconciliation: moving people closer to glorifying God by living in right relationship with God, with self, with others, and with the rest of creation" (61, 78). Ministering to the poor through acts of service, important as they are, is only one way we can restore relationships in God's kingdom. Whatever way God leads you as parents to live out the deeds of the kingdom, remember that it's relational, not just material.

## Appendix 1: Dedicated to Marriage

1. Timothy Keller, *The Meaning of Marriage: Facing the Complexities of Commitment with the Wisdom of God* (New York: Riverhead Trade, 2013), 14.
2. Shaunti Feldhahn, *The Surprising Secrets of Highly Happy Marriages: The Little Things That Make a Big Difference* (Colorado Springs: Multnomah, 2013) and *The Good News about Marriage* (Colorado Springs: Multnomah, 2014).

3. Feldhahn, *The Good News about Marriage*, 21. According to 2009 US Census Bureau data, 72 percent of people are still married to their first spouse. Yes, you read that right! And even when second and third marriages are included, the current prevalence of divorce among the general population is somewhere around 30 percent! Shaunti Feldhahn, *The Surprising Secrets of Highly Happy Marriages: The Little Things That Make a Big Difference*, Kindle ed., (Doubleday), 2109–11.

4. Feldhahn, *The Good News about Marriage*, 53.

5. Ibid., 131.

6. Ibid., 77.

7. This point is accented by the subtitle of Feldhahn's *The Surprising Secrets of Highly Happy Marriages: The Little Things That Make a Big Difference*.

8. We recommend resources such as *Love and Respect* by Emerson Eggerich and have seen marriages impacted as we've led groups at our churches through his materials. We also encourage couples to invest time and money in marriage-building events, such as the Weekend to Remember event led by FamilyLife ministry.